MORE PRAISE FOR *SOFT-BOILED*

"In tackling a subject as ever-present and fraught as masculinity, it's easy for writers to retreat to the two poles of the conversation: romance or ridicule. All the more remarkable, then, that Stephen J. West dances around that trap, with prose that is wry and funny and skeptical, but also deeply heartfelt and true. *Soft-Boiled* leaves no stone unturned in its investigation of this unified myth of American manhood, and Stephen J. West is a smart, fun, kind-hearted investigator, willing—like Frank Streets, the enigma at the book's center—to let us ride along and see what happens next."

—Lucas Mann, author of *Lord Fear*

"This beguiling hybrid of a book had me entranced from start to finish, and left me pondering not just the stories we tell ourselves about what it means to be a man in America, but the art of storytelling itself."

—Brian Gresko, editor of *When I First Held You: 22 Critically Acclaimed Writers Talk about the Triumphs, Challenges, and Transformative Experience of Fatherhood*

soft-BOILED

An Investigation of Masculinity & the Writer's Life

STEPHEN J. WEST

Kristen!
So great to share
this writing life
with you —
Thank you
for supporting
me :)

SJW

kelson
books

Kelson Books
Portland, Oregon

Published by KELSON BOOKS
2033 SE Lincoln, Portland, Oregon 97214
kelsonbooks@gmail.com

Cover design by Libby VanWhy
Interior design by Steve Connell | *steveconnell.net*

Kelson Books are printed on paper from certified sustainable forestry practices.

Printed in the United States of America.

ISBN 978-0-9827838-7-0

Library of Congress Control Number: 2022933544

For Rip–

It has become customary in Books About Men to hang one's hat on an archetype chosen from myth or story. I think this is a fine custom.

—R. W. Connell, *Masculinities*

My eyes darted among the faces behind the glass of the security checkpoint. I looked down at El, his form curved to my own beneath the carrier that held him tightly to my chest. His eyes were pink and bleary, and the corners of his mouth were crusted with the formula I'd been mixing for him in airport bathrooms. We'd been strapped to each other for the better part of eighteen hours. His blanket was damp, and his shirt, like mine, was stained with spit-up and sweet with the smell of urine.

I looked for K's heart-shaped face among the crowd, waiting for that glimpse of freckles and glowing eyes that would mark the return of the support El and I needed.

I had convinced her I could do it, that I could travel to Oaxaca, Mexico, with our nine-month-old in the middle of her research trip, that I could bear the responsibility of being a primary parent to support her and the book she was writing. I had convinced myself that I could do it.

But that was before El and I nearly missed our flight because he wasn't listed on my boarding pass; before I learned that a man traveling alone with an infant is more likely a human trafficker than a father; before I raced through the terminal to reach our gate just in time, no time to change his diaper, its spongy yellow mass already having soaked his onesie; before I muffled his tantrum in the crook of my neck while we waited for our connecting flight, the other travelers eying the wild rhythm of my dancing as I tried to soothe him through a series of delays;

before El soiled his diaper so heavily on our final flight that it soaked both of us and I didn't even think of changing him because he was sleeping; before our stiff and silent embrace was broken by the circuit board of Oaxaca that materialized among the murky desert beneath us; before I struggled to explain in broken Spanish to the stoic Mexican immigration officer that our car seat hadn't arrived, his eyes moving back and forth between El and the space behind me as they searched for the woman he expected to be in charge of this baby, his eyes finally resting on mine with the question of exactly what kind of man I was, wearing a whimpering baby and panicking about a car seat.

I was already concerned I couldn't commit myself to being a family man, before El and I stumbled into the humid Oaxaca air, before I found K and our eyes locked, before my muscles gave out as I passed our son to her and he smiled and giggled and squealed through his stupor. Before I exhaled for the first time.

I clutched El in the backseat of our beat-up rental car as K drove through the narrow, potholed streets toward our hacienda. I thought about the opportunity I'd just left behind in West Virginia. I thought about Frank Streets.

"It was a ghost hunt," Frank Streets said when I last visited him in his office. "They said, oh my god, he's involved in all of these cases—the cop in Shinnston, the sheriff in Barbour County, the suicide in Clarksburg. Let's see what he's got, and the only way they could raid my place was with a felony charge. I told you from the word go, I'm the only private investigator in this state that will go against prosecutors or law enforcement. No one else wants to get involved. It was a ghost hunt," he said with determined eyes. "It really was."

I had been shadowing Frank Streets on several cases for the better part of a year, and he had just been indicted on felony charges—five days before El and I left for Oaxaca.

But I get ahead of myself.

Before I could wish I was on a ghost hunt instead of being

a supportive husband and father abroad, before the arrest of a private investigator in West Virginia could come to represent my last, best chance to become the man I always desired myself to be—a writer smirking with the secrets of the world—I had to meet Frank Streets.

I pulled into a gravel driveway off Valley View Road and parked my car. I sat with the engine idling. 10:14 am. The scene was still: a house, a driveway, a carport, a deck, and a yard. It wasn't an office complex like I had expected, no flickering neon sign for Investigation Division, Inc., and no mention of Frank Streets anywhere. It was just another house on a backroad amidst the stippled geography of West Virginia.

I stepped out of my car and looked around. I left the doors unlocked. If Frank Streets was profiling me from behind a cracked blind or on a closed-circuit camera, I wanted to appear as professional as possible, show him I had nothing to hide and nothing to fear. I made my way up the driveway, my feet chattering on the loose gravel. I walked up to the sliding glass door, knocked softly, and opened it. I stretched my head in and looked around.

"Hello?" I squawked. The room was still. No sign of a private investigator anywhere—or an office—just a room layered from floor to ceiling with taxidermied animals and assault rifles of all shapes and sizes. I held my breath, my head protruding through the cracked sliding glass door like a bust ready to be mounted. This can't be the right place, this absolutely cannot be the right place, I thought, convinced that a red laser sight was trembling on my temple. I had messed up the directions—I should have listened to Frank Streets more closely—this wasn't Valley View Road at all, and I was stupidly intruding on some mountain man's safe house, a space he would undoubtedly defend with brutal force. K knew I was headed to meet Frank Streets, but she had no idea where he lived. Frozen there, my eyes darted among the nature-themed carpets, wallpaper, and window treatments. The lampshades were camouflaged, and the blinds were camouflaged. I saw a pool table littered with camouflaged assault rifles and camouflaged hunting gear. There were two stuffed turkeys standing in the middle of the room, several deer busts mounted on the walls, fish flailing in midair, a smattering of grouse and pheasant and quail flapping, nesting, and cuckooing on every surface. A bobcat swatted its paw and snarled from a distant corner; a fox perked and pointed with his neck extended, one paw dangling flaccidly. Cabinets displayed framed hunting photos, decorative patches, and medals. Statuettes carved out of wood and fungi were cluttered on flat surfaces. And tucked into every last nook and cranny were animal pelts, antlers, and unidentifiable skeletal remains. I wondered where among the dead animals my body would be stuffed, mounted, and displayed, a trophy with mouth agape and marbled eyes that swirled with the unanswered question, How the hell had I gotten myself into this mess?

A man emerged from my left, breaking the spell—but he didn't shoot me. He didn't even have a gun. But my suspicion was confirmed: whoever ruled this bunker was a bear of a human. I gathered my wits and realized, that, thank goodness, this might be Frank Streets. I had seen pictures of him on the website for Investigation Divisions, Inc., and knew he was an imposing figure, but he was taller and heavier than I had expected. The room felt smaller with him in it, and he looked out of place among the décor; his black slacks and polished shoes, short-sleeve button-up shirt, gold braided bracelet and necklace were not the attire I imagined the man who murdered me in this room would be wearing. This was a businessman, and the meeting we were about to have was business.

"You Stephen? Frank Streets," the bear-man said, grabbing and shaking my hand firmly as I tiptoed into the room and closed the door behind me. My hands are not small, even if they are susceptible to blistering. But grasped in Frank Streets's calloused paw, my hand looked girlish, like he might crush every bone in it on accident. I demurely looked up at his thicket of salt-and-pepper hair shaved short on the sides and gelled into a crew cut. His beard was silvering like his hair and trimmed into a neat goatee, and his eyes were wide set and crowded by thick eyebrows that ran flat across his face. His mouth was nearly as wide as his jaw. Frank Streets is a handsome man, and I'd like to say his face is shaped like a V, but it's not true. He's no hard-boiled private dick; he is a man made of obtuse angles, not the stuff dreamed up in a hard-boiled novel.

And I am certainly no knockout dame; I looked shabby and small in the jeans, flannel shirt, and hiking boots I chose to help mask the obvious: I'm not from 'round here.

"People must get lost all the time coming to your office, because you gave really good directions," I offered with a giggle.

"I always tell people their GPS thingies won't work down here, but they try it anyway and end up getting lost," Frank Streets replied, shaking his head like a beleaguered teacher whose students keep making the same mistakes.

Frank Streets and I talked about his family's long history working as coal miners and how he had started in the mines during high school. We talked about his military service and deployment to Germany during the Gulf War, and about how it ended with an honorable discharge because of a mysterious nervous-system ailment that might have come from "getting into some stuff we shouldn't have." He described his brief stint as a sheriff's deputy in Barbour County that ended when he couldn't stomach the way justice was consistently compromised by corruption. He explained how the military helped him get a two-year degree and how he vowed he would never go back to school—and then immediately put himself through college at Fairmont State to earn his bachelor-of-science degree in criminal justice. He proudly told me how he used that education to become a licensed private investigator and, in the early nineties, founded Investigation Division, Inc., a firm with multiple employees that works up to twenty cases at a time.

He told me about his ability to administer polygraphs, how he was a certified tactical-weapon and combat instructor, and how he had worked as a bounty hunter capturing fugitives and parole jumpers for a while before settling into private investigation. He said he had lost count of how many times he'd had a fist, a knife, or a gun pulled on him, how many battered and abused women he'd seen, how many pairs of semen-covered underwear he had stored in Ziplock bags in the filing cabinets in his office, or how many victims with bullet holes in their skulls he'd taken pictures of.

I was on Valley View Road looking for something to write about, and West-By-God-Virginia, I'd hit a fucking gold mine with this guy. Or maybe a coal seam would be apropos.

"You ever seen covert cameras?" Frank Streets asked as he rose from behind his thick oak desk.

"No, I haven't. Do you have one?" He waved me over to a door near the entrance to his office. This was a narrow, cramped space, like a hallway or walk-in closet, and the walls were lined with filing cabinets and desks covered with paperwork. It was barely wide enough for Frank Streets to walk through without his upper body scraping along each side as he went.

On the wall just to the right of the entrance to the room, he had a collection of a dozen or so framed images of famous detectives and private investigators, most of which were of Sherlock Holmes. Among them were photographs of actors who had played the iconic detective in movies and television series, and illustrations that I could only guess were reprints of old book covers. Frank Streets beamed at me in front of his collection.

"Here's me and Peter Falk," he announced proudly, pointing at an image near the middle of the collection.

"Cool. Who's that?"

"You don't know who Peter Falk is?" I shook my head sheepishly.

Frank Streets glared. "He played Colombo on TV. I got to meet him at a national private investigators conference. He was the keynote."

I had heard of *Colombo* and thought about telling him that, but I didn't want to sound patronizing. I wish I could have validated his enthusiasm in that moment, to show him that I understood his collection in a fundamental way. I couldn't connect with his capturing a fugitive or collecting other people's semen-covered clothing—hell, I'd never even shot a gun—but Frank Streets and I weren't so different. We were lifelong approximations of the men we longed to be, too deep into our performances to turn back now: Frank Streets, a small-time private investigator in the middle of nowhere trying to crack every case like the world depended on it; and me, an adjunct instructor with a spouse, a son, and student-debt payments to make still hanging on to the dream that I could be a writer, grinning with self-satisfied accomplishment from the back of a book like those I displayed in my office.

After Frank Streets showed me his collection of cameras tucked into everything from the bill of a baseball cap to the clip of a ballpoint pen, we left his office and went back into the room with the animal skins and weaponry. Instead of escorting me to the sliding glass door, he stopped in the middle of the room and looked at me expectantly.

"This is my den," he said finally. "Designed it myself."

"It's really amazing—there's so much . . . stuff in here. I've never seen this many stuffed animals in one place before." I swallowed hard. I'd just described his collection of taxidermied kills as "stuffed animals." Frank Streets didn't seem to mind as he proudly surveyed his lair.

"Yep. Got them all myself. Except that albino grouse on the wall over there. My son-in-law got that one." I looked where he nodded but couldn't tell which bird he meant. "I built this den when I was gonna retire a couple years back—but I never did," he said wistfully. "My wife said I had to retire if I built it, but I just keep on taking cases." His eyes flashed at me and a smirk curled in the corner of his mouth.

The room looked less like a den for a retiree than it did a natural history museum. Actually, it looked more like a natural history museum that was shut down and moved into a 200-square-foot storage space. The highlight of it all—even more so than the diversity of fauna frozen around the room— was the wallpaper on the largest wall, which featured a scene of a glade with a babbling brook and regal buck, not unlike murals painted on the sides of conversion vans from the 1970s.

"I had the wallpaper imported from California," he boasted.

So, this is Frank Streets: an intimidatingly large man, former coal miner, former military, former sheriff's deputy, licensed to teach the most effective way to subdue a person with a baton, and a thoughtful interior decorator. The space wasn't just a mishmash of a trophy room designed to celebrate Frank Streets as a prolific sportsman, it was a monument to his self-actualized manhood, designed with an artist's eye.

I could cut Frank Streets down here and conclude that his identity as an outdoorsman was reductive, that he wanted me to admire his manliness, but I could see through his hunting prowess to the expression of fragility it represented. Lo, the phallus goes boom, and the bodies of animals are rendered proof of virility.

But I am no better.

What kind of man am I? What wallpaper would I hang in my den?

I needed Frank Streets: his booming persona and harrowing life as a private investigator were the muse I was missing in my conventional, middle-class life.

After some chitchat about the attributes of the assault rifles on the pool table, Frank Streets walked me outside and told me about a day he filmed two people having sex in the backseat of a car, how he walked right up to the window with his video recorder in broad daylight. He described how the man jumped out of the car and pulled the woman out by her hair, how her knees were scuffed and bloodied as she got up cussing and taking swings at him, while the man, still fully naked and "dripping with sex," grabbed a tire iron out of his trunk. Frank Streets escaped the situation by coolly pulling out his sidearm and saying, "Whoa there, buddy."

"If I hadn't had the gun on me, he would have beaten me to a pulp with that tire iron, so I always pack heat," he said as he leaned over and spit out some chewing tobacco around the side of his house, the sun reflecting off his silver belt buckle and shined black leather shoes.

"Frank, if I can ask—can I shadow you sometime—ride along with you on one of your cases. You know, to write about it?" This was why I'd driven to Valley View Road. This was why I needed Frank Streets. "I'll buy you a steak dinner," I squawked, the sweat beading on my forehead as I tried to hold eye contact with him.

"Sassy!" he yelped. It took a second to register that he was yelling at the Chihuahua a few yards off and not me. "Sassy, get outta there, go on." She looked up at Frank Streets with weepy eyes and continued chewing on a chunk of poop that was twice as thick as her leg. "Stupid dog—Sassy, stop it!" he said gruffly to the dog and swatted in her direction, but I could tell he intended no harm as he leaned over, cantilevered by one giant leg, swiftly scooped Sassy up, and tucked her in the crook of his arm.

"You can background check me if you want, you know, if that makes you feel more comfortable." I gulped, trying to galvanize the soft curve of my desire. Frank Streets smiled and crossed his arms.

"That won't be necessary," he said as Sassy settled into his massive embrace, a position she was clearly familiar with. Frank Streets beamed as Sassy licked her chops and gave her head a brisk shake, her pink sequined collar sparkling in the early spring sun.

❋

"You're gonna do great," K assured me from the front steps of our home in Morgantown as I walked to the car through the morning twilight. "Take lots of notes and pictures—and don't forget to turn the recorder on!"

Frank Streets and I were about to spend the day together. There was a significant chance we could spend the next ten hours sitting in a parked truck waiting for a suspected adulterer to leave his home, with no guarantee he would. Other than that, I had no clue what the day would reveal.

K had a practical understanding of how I should approach my time shadowing Frank Streets that I did not. As a political scientist, her writing relies upon anecdotal observations she gathers through field research, and over the years I'd known her she routinely traveled to remote areas of Latin America to observe political candidates on the campaign trail, following them into the Amazon basin or Andean highlands as they dish out baby chickens or prescription medications to buy the votes needed to win election. The most extensive field research I'd ever done besides hang out in the bar with my friend Ben and blather about my big ideas for this or that book I was going to write was when K took me to a Mexican beach resort just a short drive across the border from her home in Tucson, where she ordered fish tacos and margaritas in perfect Spanish and rented an ATV for me to nervously drive us around on in the desert.

I needed her guidance and emotional support. Not to mention she was the primary breadwinner in our household. Her salary exceeded mine, and without it I wouldn't have had the privilege to commit myself to the more elaborate larks she encouraged me to chase.

And she knew how to write a book. The research she had conducted in the field produced not one but two complete book manuscripts. K understands the importance of having a purpose behind the research a writer conducts, and a clear, urgent question that the researcher is in pursuit of an answer to. A reason for studying human subjects. The essentialness of a purpose for observing and reporting on a private investigator, for example.

"What if he asks you why you want to ride along with him? He'll know you are there watching him for a reason." I could hear K's voice in my head. So. What is your reason for observing Frank Streets?

I'd heard this question from writer friends, too, when I brought up my idea to write about a private investigator.

In a craft essay from 1947 George Orwell defines four fundamental reasons people choose to write: historical impulse, political purpose, aesthetic enthusiasm, and sheer egoism. The first week of the intro to creative writing class I teach, I have students shuffle off to separate corners of the room depending on which of the four impulses they most strongly identify with. I feel a twinge of shame when I sidle over to join the sheer-egoism group, knowing that Orwell explains this impulse as "the desire to seem clever, to be talked about, to be remembered after death, to get your own back on the grownups who snubbed you in childhood." With that, the morning sheets are stripped off my persona in the classroom, exposing to the chill air of my students' judgment what I deep down believe is a shitty and self-serving reason for making art. And sheer egoism is the smallest group in the room every semester. Maybe it's because it actually is a shitty reason to make art. But I tell my little group that their honesty about their egos is winning, because as Orwell writes, "it is humbug to pretend this is not a motive." And I assure them that our cohort is really much bigger than it appears: most people put public persona ahead of private truth because it feels safer. Especially writers.

"I give all this background information," Orwell parries after sharing a forgettable early poem that reveals his youthful allegiance to aesthetic enthusiasm, "because I do not think one can assess a writer's motives without knowing something of his early development. His subject matter will be determined by the age he lives in—at least this is true in tumultuous, revolutionary ages like our own—but before he ever begins to write he will have acquired an emotional attitude from which he will never completely escape."

Orwell concludes the essay with a challenge. "It seems to me nonsense, in a period like our own, to think that one can avoid writing of such subjects."

Orwell was referring to the rise of fascism in Europe between the world wars, the "subject matter" that he could not avoid writing about in *Animal Farm* and *1984* despite his fundamental desire to compose inert poems about the beauty of a glade in spring rain.

And I believe his challenge stands. It is nonsense to think that certain subjects can be avoided in a period like our own.

I heard from a friend who once took a workshop with Jenny Boully that she challenged the group of writers, "If what you are writing doesn't feel dangerous, then why write?"

"A work of art is good if it has arisen out of necessity," Rilke writes in *Letters to a Young Poet*. "That is the only way one can judge it."

So . . . riding along with Frank Streets feels dangerous. See: the collection of assault rifles that he peruses like a kid surveying flavors in an ice cream parlor before choosing one to take to work. But who wants to read about my fear of dying? Freud covered that. Who wants to read about my childhood? I am Oedipus, and a story of my early life does not feel dangerous nor sprung from necessity.

"Why can't you be explicit about that fact? That you are searching for something to write about?" my friend Torrey challenged me when I shared that I didn't think I had anything worth writing about. "I think it would be a window into who you actually are."

But, Torrey, listen: I'm uninteresting at a macro level. I am from western New York. My parents never divorced and still live in the same house I grew up in. I did well in school and was popular. I'm healthy, pretty good looking (sheer egoism), and reasonably athletic. I'm young(ish), heterosexual, married with children, have multiple college degrees, and am fully employed. I am what sociologist Erving Goffman would call "the one unblushing male in America."

"You are a white man." Torrey stated obviously, and I cringed. Even without her label being presented as negative, it made me uncomfortable, which mattered. "Why don't you dig into that?"

I had read a few articles on gender theory in graduate school that amounted to the Goodreads top quotes from Judith Butler's *Gender Trouble*. I learned how gender is socially constructed, how we all perform versions of masculinity and femininity that have been modeled to us by our culture, ways of acting as women and men that are in line with what society expects. I believe this theory, see it in myself, but I still felt uncomfortable by Torrey's simple acknowledgment of who I am when reduced to a one-line bio. I felt the involuntary squirt of cortisol hit like it does when I join my sheer egoism group in class, blushing over my immense privilege, my lack of anything traumatic or dangerous or novel to write about being laid bare, and the shame that my straight, coastal, American, white maleness—my position at the ivory tower of privilege— my embarrassment of riches—my self—was not something to draw attention to. Was in fact something to avoid in writing. It was something that needed an alibi.

In a period like our own. Why don't you dig into that.

"Throughout American History," Michael Kimmel writes in *Manhood in America*, a book I found once I started to dig, "American men have been afraid that others will see us as less than manly, as weak, timid, frightened. And men have been afraid of not measuring up to some vaguely defined notions of what it means to be a man, afraid of failure."

Me, the one unblushing American male. Yet I blush, dear reader. I blush for my desire to matter more than my privilege. I blush for my need to make art, even when my art is not needed. I blush because Frank Streets springs from that necessity.

"Take good notes—and don't forget to call!" K said after one more wave goodbye. I rolled my eyes for her like an angsty tween. She folded her arms like a put-upon housewife. The look she shot me was one I'd seen countless times, beginning almost a decade earlier at a Halloween party in Iowa City.

"I like your haircut," I had offered casually over my shoulder that night as I strolled by, making sure to catch her eyes as I sashayed in my excruciatingly child-sized Ninja Turtle costume (Michelangelo, obvs). Her dark natural ringlets—the way they framed her freckled and heart-shaped face, her flirty smile—had made an impression on me when I first saw her in a class I visited as a prospective graduate student months before.

K tells people that she remembers me visiting that class, remembers walking with me in a group to the Airliner for pizza afterward, then to the Deadwood for cheap beer, how I made sure to make eye contact with her when I said goodbye. She wants to remember because it's a perfect little meet-cute origin story for our romance, but I know she doesn't because when I walked away from her at that Halloween party, her sapphire eyes beamed with concern and curiosity, with the who-the-hell-is-this-guy look I'd hoped for. But the thing in her look that startled me, the feeling I keep going back for, was the impression that she could see more of me than I was comfortable revealing, like there was nothing I could hide from her—not my fragile ego, not my fear of failing—not even the conclusion that I was going to call her before I ever had her number.

I pulled into the Staples parking lot and drove to the back as Frank Streets had instructed me to. The space I parked in was facing the only entrance.

I cut the engine, took a deep breath, and settled into my seat. I squinted into the morning sunlight that refracted through the windshield. Thank goodness for the clear day. I was anxious, and waiting in an empty parking lot with the kind of gray drizzle that seeps into your marrow would have pushed me over the edge.

Before I settled into my space in the Staples lot to wait for Frank Streets, I had a few minutes to spare, so I pulled into the Go-Mart nestled just down the road between Applebee's and Walmart. I walked to the coolers at the back of the store and stared hard at the cornucopia of bottled drinks. Frank Streets mentioned a couple of times on the phone the night before that along with a handful of other essentials—granola bars, a thermos of coffee, Kodiak wintergreen snuff—he makes sure to bring his pee bottle when he's working a case. He told me to bring mine, as if I already had one designated for duty.

"Yup, of course," I'd replied. I didn't want to make it weird by asking too many questions about pee bottles.

Peeing in a bottle is usually an act of necessity, one essentially performed only by males. I have no doubt women have peed in bottles throughout history, but there is little dispute that the male anatomy lends itself more naturally to the act. But that ergonomic advantage gets complicated, as so many things do—most things, really—by the instinct men have to use their penises for cheap laughs. I've only peed in a bottle once in my life, as a teenager in the backseat of a car on a road trip with friends. I didn't really have to pee in the bottle, but it helped stave off the tedium of the drive.

Can a pee bottle be any old bottle that's lying around? Would glass or plastic be better? Should it be opaque to avoid making a bold display of one's urine? Is it manly to urinate less, both in terms of frequency and volume? And, if yes, is any capacity for a pee bottle over twelve ounces a faux pas of gender norms? I have to admit that I have the uncanny ability to pee more liquid than I actually take in. Is it emasculating to have to empty one's pee bottle mid-stakeout—let alone mid-stream? What does it say about me if I bring a two-liter bottle? "My penis is average size, but I sure can piss a lot!"

After weighing the merits of various brands and sizes, I settled on Gatorade for my pee bottle. It was simple, really: functional without the insinuation of self-consciousness, a vessel that can survive a fall, that won't make that crinkling sound when my hand is shaking and I'm battling stage fright in the cab of Frank Streets's Durango. I imagined the deep thrum of confidence my pee would evoke as it pounded the inside of the bottle. This is the image I wanted to portray to Frank Streets: a man who knows what he is doing, confident with who he is and what he's about, with no qualms about publicly peeing in a bottle, let alone choosing one for the job.

Maybe the necessity of the pee bottle in private investigation accounts for the scarcity of female detectives. At least it makes sense for their absence from the literary record, as everyone is painfully aware that male writers are obsessed with penises.

Frank Streets pulled into the Staples parking lot and headed toward me, cutting diagonally across the grid of parking spaces, the six-foot CB antenna mounted on its roof still swaying as the vehicle came to a stop. I unbuckled quickly and jumped out of my car, suddenly conscious that the hue of my Honda Fit that the salesman called "blackberry pearl" was sparkling in the morning sunlight.

"Sorry I'm a little late," he said, his thigh-sized arm dangling halfway down the door of his Durango.

"Oh, I just got here not long ago myself," I lied as Frank Streets clambered out, the truck lurching under his shifting mass. We shook hands and made furtive eye contact.

"Is it alright if I bring my bag along?" I had a few things in my satchel that I wanted to have with me: a peanut butter and jelly sandwich, my camera, an audio recorder, and my freshly emptied pee bottle.

"Sure, just let me move some stuff around back here." Frank Streets opened the rear passenger door to shift his equipment around on the backseat. He was wearing black cargo fatigues, hiking boots, a short-sleeve plaid button-down shirt, and what looked like a beige fishing vest with every pocket stuffed full. His large silver watch flashed as he shuffled around some duffle bags in the backseat. I noticed his gun peeking out from under the fishing vest—a black pistol holstered to his belt, just behind a gold and silver badge. I expected the gun, but I had no idea what that badge could mean. In my experience, these were items reserved for sheriffs and marshals or for kids playing cops and robbers. It looked real, but I didn't dare lean in to read what it said. I was as close to that gun as I wanted to be. I grabbed my camera, threw my bag in the backseat, climbed up front, and buckled in.

We left the shopping center and drove. I had no clue where we were going, and I wasn't about to ask. Frank Streets and I barely talked as I watched him navigate fluidly through uninhabited backroads without a map or "GPS thingy."

After about fifteen minutes, he nodded his head slightly toward his window.

"There it is," he said as we continued driving at the same speed.

"There is what?" I didn't see anything through his window—just a trailer park spilling into the valley in the distance.

"The subject's house." Frank Streets pointed again with his chin, "Through there, through the trees, the white house on top of the hill above that trailer park." The house he pointed to was barely visible as we flew by it, but I could make out the one he was referring to, a large white colonial-style home with green shutters and a charcoal-colored Toyota Tacoma parked in front of the garage.

"What, who's the subject?"

"Suspected adulterer," Frank Streets replied out of the side of his mouth. "That's his truck there—looks like he's still home." What I could see of the subject's house was nicer than I had anticipated for a suspected adulterer—at least the suspected adulterer I imagined we were going to watch in rural West Virginia. I expected ramshackle, yard clutter. This was a suburban split-level set back from the street, with simple landscaping, a paved driveway. In that way, it did stand out among the overgrowth and dirt driveways I'd seen along the drive there, but it wasn't remarkable.

As we reached the top of a hill about a quarter mile from the subject's house, Frank Streets slowed down and pulled a

U-turn into a gravelly wide spot, put the truck in park and turned off the ignition. The sun streamed through the windshield as silence engulfed the cab of the Durango. It was a little after seven on the kind of brisk morning made for a steaming mug of coffee and a newspaper, maybe even a relaxing drive through the countryside. My seat squeaked awkwardly as I settled in.

We had parked near the entrance to the Harmony Valley Retirement Community, and just a few yards from a small church that obstructed most of our view of the trailers that collected like discarded Tic Tacs in the crease of the valley to our right. The sign on the side of the road said SUN VALLEY, UNINCORPORATED. I wasn't sure if that was the name of the town, the church, or the road. We had as much of a view as you can get in this part of West Virginia, where vistas are quickly snuffed out by the overlapping hills that extend in every direction. We couldn't see the subject's house, but we could see the driveway, and that was apparently all we needed.

The road was quiet; only two cars had passed us in the first ten minutes of our stakeout. As I sat watching the driveway, I felt nervous that what we might discover could very well spell the demise of a marriage. We were looking to ruin someone's life, I thought. Many people's lives—if they had kids, I mean, and I didn't even know their names. Frank Streets let out a large exhale, and I wondered what the pit of his stomach felt like.

Most of the cases Frank Streets takes involve events in people's personal lives that are damaging, usually due to infidelity, drugs, stealing, running away, or lying about any number of things. Before he takes a case, he spends time in his office mining into his clients, into the details of their relationships, everything from their daily routines to the last time they slept with their significant other. For the case we were currently working on, the client had even brought Frank Streets a pair of her husband's dirty underwear that she had pinched from the laundry basket.

In some ways, being a private investigator is like being a therapist; both are burdened with a client's desire for resolution to a problem. The main difference between a therapist and a private investigator is that in one context resolution is pursued inwardly and in the other it is pursued outwardly. The therapist finds resolution by encouraging a client to become the subject of self-investigation, to evaluate what lies within themself so they can uncover the truth and in so doing enable themself to move forward. While the process of the PI is similarly inspired, it is fundamentally opposed. The PI finds resolution for a client by investigating the actions of others and uncovering the truth about them, enabling the client to then move forward. When someone hires a therapist, they become the agent of their own resolution. When someone hires a PI, they grant agency over that resolution to someone else. That is the main difference I can see. That and PIs pack heat.

"It's a lot of responsibility you have—I mean, what you see, what you find out on a job like this affects the foundation of people's lives, the identities they've crafted for themselves, years in the making. Not that it's your responsibility that their relationships are messed up, I mean—either there is a problem or there isn't. It's just that you are kind of responsible in some way, if you find something out, I mean. That's heavy." I cringed.

"It is," Frank Streets replied sincerely, as if he'd been thinking the same thing. I widened an eyelid and looked over at him. "To have a client come and pour her guts out to you—I mean about everything—it makes me wanna catch the subject. I get real mad when I don't. If he's not up to anything, that's fine. But if he is, I wanna find out."

Frank Streets's desire was tangible. I wanted to catch the subject, too, but my desire felt less noble. The faster the subject drove, the better; the more beautiful or bizarre his mistress, the better; if he had a gun and pulled it out, screaming, "I'm gonna kill everyone," the better; if a karate fight between Frank Streets and the subject broke out, the better; and if I was somehow able to overcome my debilitating fear to subdue the subject with a crane kick, disarming him and pointing the gun in his face with a manly growl that dared him to "go ahead and try me," the best.

I wanted so badly to have a day worth writing about with Frank Streets that it revealed what was incomplete about my analogy of therapy and investigation: I had excluded myself. If a therapist, a PI, and a writer were all working the same case, the writer would be the one selfishly looking for a punch line while the other two got down to problem solving. I was out there with Frank Streets to find something to write about because . . . because I wanted something to write about. I could feel Rilke's eyes roll across space and time. "Go into yourself," he would say after biting his lip for a bit. "Search for the reason that bids you write; find out whether it is spreading out its roots in the deepest places of your heart, acknowledge to yourself whether you would have to die if it were denied you to write." I slumped in the cab of the Durango with no subject in sight and nowhere to go. Fulfilling my desire to make art worth dying for felt as likely as finding a needle in a haystack. I wasn't a writer, and I certainly wasn't special. I was just another guy sitting in a truck in West Virginia.

For Kimmel, the dominant form of American manhood that we know today took shape among the first generation of men after the American Revolution. Freed from British rule and the cultural influence it had on them, this generation of men embraced identities that evolved from a revision of the two main categories of colonial masculinity: first, the independent and virtuous "man's man," a craftsman by trade, an honest, hard worker defined by self-reliance and the skill of his labor; second, the aristocratic public gentleman, an effete intellectual with wigs and ruffles, concerned with cosmopolitan tastes and cultured sensibilities, his relationships to family, church, and community, and ultimately his status in social encounters.

When I think of the founding fathers, my mind flickers with a mash-up of incongruent images: the George Washingtons and Samuel Adamses and Benjamin Franklins and Thomas Jeffersons, bewigged and powdered and buttoned up with just dandy wool suits as they cross rivers and shoot down British soldiers, as they till fields and chop down cherry trees and build log cabins and whip and impregnate slaves on their plantations for the idea of an America rooted in soil rich with blood from black and Native bodies, all set to the tune of a fancy harpsichord and genteel applause. It makes me wonder how these founding fathers would be received if they rolled up to a bar in West Virginia one evening. Would their wigs and heavy makeup and prim clothes be cool because of the grime under their fingernails from the day's toil in the fields? Or would they be unmanly because of their concern for refined beauty?

The status quo expression of masculinity that we recognize today evolved from a combination of both versions of colonial manhood. This authentic American brand of manhood was defined by a man's participation in the public sphere, his accumulated wealth and status, his social mobility, his aggressiveness and competitiveness. This is the "Self-Made Man" that continues to dominate the American male psyche to this day.

I participate in the public sphere . . . reluctantly. I attend social gatherings that K says I have to attend. I want to be more involved in the arts community, to be a familiar face at readings and gallery openings, but I'm usually too anxious to actually go. Sure, you say, but social media! The Twenty-first Century! You have a phone and a thumb, so you can participate! Not that I do all that well. I have seventy-four Twitter followers, and I last updated my Facebook profile ten years ago.

Alongside the emergence of the Self-Made Man, the term *breadwinner* came into usage around the middle of the nineteenth century to describe the actions associated with the role a man played in the domestic sphere—and the importance of that being observed publicly. Men began measuring their manhood by their ability to earn and provide both at home and in civic duties. Breadwinning became the most important measure of the achievement of the Self-Made Man. It was this virtue that men became anxious that other men see and acknowledge.

And there is pressure that comes with manhood being acknowledged publicly—by men, for men. As Kimmel observes, "the Self-Made Man was also temperamentally restless, chronically insecure, and desperate to achieve a solid grounding for a masculine identity."

More like The Self-Questioning Man. This is a masculinity that I identify with.

Imagine a charcoal Toyota Tacoma driving casually down its driveway on a Saturday morning in early spring. When the subject's truck appeared, the moment was even more mundane than that. But it was something, and as I watched the truck roll down the driveway, I waited a second, expecting Frank Streets to jolt to life, shaking the car as he jammed his foot on the pedal, screaming into the CB, "The bald eagle has flown the nest"—but he didn't. He hadn't seen the truck yet. He was looking down at his video recorder. I had to do something or this whole charade would be over before it had even begun. I gulped and said aloud softly, like lines rehearsed in a high school hallway before an audition:

"There's the truck."

Frank Streets's head snapped up. "Ah! There's the truck— he's going!" The Durango's chassis creaked awake as Frank Streets rumbled to life, stabbing at the CB with one hand, buckling his seatbelt with the other, and jerking the ignition. He adjusted himself in his seat again, using the wheel for leverage to thrust his body forward. My eyes were locked on the subject's truck as it rolled to a gentle stop at the end of his driveway, turned into the empty right lane of Sun Valley Road, and drove away just as innocently as could be.

Frank Streets barked into the CB. "Subject is leaving and heading toward you. Over. He's driving toward you! I'm pulling out now — I'll catch up to him, and then you get behind me. We can't lose sight of him!"

We hastily pulled out into the road, the Durango's cylinders screaming as the tires kicked up gravel. I was stunned by how aggressively Frank Streets took to the chase, given we were still clearly visible in the truck's rearview mirror, being no more than a quarter mile back. I imagined the subject must have noticed us pull out in a cloud of dust on this otherwise empty stretch of road, one that he knows intimately. I like to think I would notice a scene like that unfolding behind me when I left my driveway. Maybe I wouldn't, though; even if I did glance back, why would I assume it had anything to do with me?

As we made up ground on the subject, Frank Streets pointed out a white Neon parked at the end of a row of white construction vehicles: his other car. I noted that there were two people seated in front as they pulled out behind us, but I couldn't discern any details of what they looked like, not even the color of their clothing.

"We don't want to draw too much attention to ourselves," Frank Streets said and eased off the gas a little. I was still thinking of the cloud of dust we kicked up and how maniacally we just drove to get to the point where we didn't want to be suspicious.

We followed the Tacoma as it leisurely wound along Sun Valley Road at just a touch under fifty-five miles per hour. Despite our initial dramatic peel out, this had turned into a low-speed chase as we vacillated between forty-five and fifty-five to stay at least a few hundred feet behind the subject. My heart pounded fiercely in spite of the low speeds. Frank Streets and I sat tensely in the car. Should I look forward? Or should I look out the window? Should Frank Streets and I talk and laugh and smile like people do, or just burn a hole in the back of the charcoal Tacoma with our laser-like stares?

We approached a four-way stop and the charcoal Tacoma

took a right onto U.S. 50.

"He's heading toward Clarksburg," Frank Streets muttered. "Just like she said he would."

"Who's she?"

"The client."

"Who's the client?"

"The subject's wife," Frank Streets added gruffly as the subject accelerated onto the highway. "His wife says he leaves every Saturday morning about this time for several hours but never says where he's going."

"She's out of town this weekend on business in New York, so we figured it was a good bet he would keep to his routine—especially with no one watching or keeping track of how long he's gone." Frank Streets's eyes gleamed. "She says he goes to Clarksburg a lot, so he's doing exactly what we suspected he would so far."

"You think he's going to meet someone?"

"We'll see, won't we?" Frank Streets turned and looked at me wryly, his upper lip curling into a sneer. He wrung his hands on the steering wheel like a masseuse just stiffed on a tip and hammered the gas to keep pace.

"Not everyone brings you brownies on your birthday." I looked over as Kevin "Heavy Kevy" Hotz grabbed his bowling ball from the return and winked at me. His face threatened to be swallowed by the girth of his neck as he pushed his glasses up the bridge of his nose. It was league night at Colonial Lanes in Iowa City, and my team, Sabotage, was up against the team from Lone Tree, a neighboring one-stoplight, many-barn town. As an outfit made up of English PhD students and creative writers, we were unsurprisingly in last place in a league dominated by blue-collar Iowans who had been bowling in the same league for decades. Because of this, any of the other bowlers acknowledging our presence—let alone offering nuanced insights into human behavior, like Heavy Kevy just had—was as rare as a Sabotage strike. Then again, an attractive young woman with black ringlets and glowing eyes had just made an unexpected cameo with a tray full of brownies. It was my birthday, and K had come with treats "for the team," but Heavy Kevy was a seasoned sleuth.

"We'll be at the Vine later if you don't have plans," K offered, her black pleather pants quieting the clap of balls on pins across the league lanes as she walked away. She was friendly with everyone on the team, and we hung out now and again in large groups, so the invite wasn't a surprise. But the brownies were. And they were for me. And she looked at me when she mentioned the Vine. Huh.

"Great, we'll be there!" Mark shouted eagerly. Mark: the best bowler on Sabotage, a dear friend in Iowa City, and K's ex-boyfriend, who had told me enough times about his continued feelings for her that I had stopped complimenting K's hair when I'd see her around.

She was just being friendly, I thought. I can go to the Vine, it's nothing, she's too smart, too attractive, too funny, but then those eyes kept finding mine at the bar that night and I had to leave and avoid her for as long as I could.

It was just under three weeks later that I pulled a folded sheet of paper out of my peacoat and handed it to K, careful to avoid eye contact as we settled into the booth in the back corner of the pub.

"I wrote this for you." An arctic blast of frigid air had descended upon the Upper Midwest, but my face and neck felt unseasonably hot as K unfolded the list titled "Reasons Not to Get Involved with Me." "It's not comprehensive," I added sincerely and rubbed my forehead, my skin balling up like rubber cement in the creases of my palm. We had arranged to meet because I had been feeling K's gravity bending me toward her and I could see her bending to mine, too.

Our circle of friends orbited around Mark, and I knew that if K and I began dating it would dramatically reshape our social lives. Graduate school in Iowa City is a fishbowl, and students can find no better escape from esoteric theory than gossiping about their friends' love lives and drawing up allegiances. We'd arranged our clandestine meeting to see if there was any fate for us other than supernova.

A smile crept across her face as she read.

"It's all true," I said frankly. Her smile was fixed.

"I know," she offered warmly. She put the list down and sipped her wine. "You might break my heart, Stephen West," she said, and when I looked at her, I couldn't imagine it.

And I still can't. K and I trust each other to what might be a dangerous degree, and we both willingly sacrifice ourselves for the benefit of the other. We have grown into adults together, and her companionship is a fortune I often feel I don't deserve. Not that I've done anything to not deserve it; sometimes I just feel like a less accomplished, less successful, and less confident man than she deserves. At least I tell her where I'm going when I leave for the day.

"We've been on his tail for a while now, we need to switch the chase vehicle," Frank Streets said as a crease took shape between his eyebrows. We had tailed the Tacoma onto U.S. 50 toward Clarksburg, and while it was early enough in the morning that the highway wasn't congested, there were still vehicles scattered between the two lanes that Frank Streets had to contend with. The subject could exit at any moment, so we had to stay closer than Frank Streets wanted to in case we needed to quickly follow him down a ramp.

"I need to get my other car to take the lead so the subject doesn't start to notice us." As I looked around, it dawned on me why Frank Streets selected a blue Dodge Durango for his work truck: nearly every vehicle on the highway was a pickup truck or SUV. "Blue Dodge Durango" was a pattern of vehicular camouflage in West Virginia that helped Frank Streets remain inconspicuous in someone's rearview mirror.

"Where you at?" Frank Streets waited a moment, holding the CB, steering with one giant paw. "Hello? Where you at?" He yelped and squinted, "I said where you at? Okay, well you need to come up here and switch so he doesn't notice we've been on his tail, he hasn't seen you at all yet. Wait—he's exiting! He's exiting, I'm gonna drive on by to the next exit, you follow him. Don't you lose him!" Frank Streets shouted.

I watched breathlessly as the charcoal Tacoma exited to our right, launching up the ramp to West Pike Street in downtown Clarksburg in slow motion. I craned my neck back to watch it for as long as I could as Frank Streets and I continued hurdling down the highway. The subject pulled up to the light at the end of the ramp and stopped. I never caught a glimpse of the white Neon before the scene was cut off as we tunneled through the underpass.

"We'll take the next exit and circle back on them," Frank Streets announced confidently. It sounded simple enough. I took a shaky breath and scanned for the next exit.

The CB radio crackled. "Subject just pulled into the Exxon on West Pike Street. Over."

"Ten-four, I'm headed there, don't lose him." The morning sky was burnished in that high contrast brightness you want to enjoy but have to squint under sunglasses to avoid.

We made a sharp turn into a cramped lot bordered by a steep potholed alley on one side and a windowless brick wall on the other. We backed into a spot with a view of the Hartland Planing Mill Company on the left, the storefront for the Hartland Construction Supply Center directly across from us, and McDonald's golden arches next door to that. We must have been close to the subject, but we had no visual because we were boxed in on both sides. All we had to go on was that the Neon could see the golden arches across from us in the distance when looking down Pike.

Frank Streets threw the truck into park and left it running. He held the CB up to his mouth. "Where you at? Can you see the subject?"

The voice crackled back, "We're parked by a bar. The High Street Lounge. Got a clear view of the Exxon and the subject."

"What's he doing?"

"He's filling up. He's wearing jean shorts and tennis shoes and a white T-shirt. Looks like he's in pretty good shape."

Frank Streets raised his eyebrows as he spoke. "He's a brown belt in karate. Also has a motorcycle, one of those little crotch rockets. Paid for it in cash." I'm not sure where brown lies on the ass-kicking color spectrum, but it must be pretty serious if it was worth noting. That coupled with the crotch rocket made the subject seem more dangerous than the soft-bellied fifty-something I imagined we were following. Frank Streets was big and had a gun, and I'm in decent shape, but I suddenly liked our chances less if this ended with the subject wielding a tire iron like a bow staff and squealing his crotch rocket's tires, all while dripping with proverbial sex. I squirmed in my seat.

"Alright, we're parked here in a lot just across from the McDonald's." Frank Streets pulled his tin of snuff out of the center console. He popped it open and pinched a glistening black wad of it between his index finger and thumb. He plunked it in his lower lip and quickly tucked it into place with his tongue. All of this took about two seconds. "Keep me posted over the radio on what he does," he added.

"Copy that."

"You want some snuff?" He asked, looking at me expectantly as he tucked the wad further down with his tongue.

"No thanks." I wished I could have said yes; I honestly considered it. Frank Streets and I might have bonded over it like men do on a cigarette break, and that's all I wanted. But I hadn't had chewing tobacco since I tried it in high school and broke into a cold sweat and needed to lie down in the bed of my friend's pickup to fend off the nausea it inspired. I didn't want to ask Frank Streets if I could lie down in his backseat for a minute while I puked my guts out.

"So, what do you think so far?" Frank Streets grinned at

me like a father might his son on take-your-child-to-work day.

"Pretty intense." He giggled at me. He could tell by looking at me that I was feeling the pressure of the experience so
far—and all we'd done was follow a truck for a few miles, lose
it, then find it again.

The radio crackled. "Subject's walking into the Exxon. He's
talking to somebody. Can't see who."

My head was spinning. "I was worried we'd lost him back
there. He—the subject—sounds like a curious character. Why
would he pay for his motorcycle in cash? That's crazy. I can't
imagine doing that." Unless I had something to hide, I thought.

"He and his wife have separate bank accounts. She didn't
even know that he bought the bike until he showed up with it.
Drove to New York to buy it." I thought about my budget and
how K and I have long discussions about whether we can order
pizza. "Apparently he does that kind of thing all the time," said
Frank Streets, punctuating with a full stop dip spit.

"Sounds like they have some marital issues," I croaked, my
throat still constricted with nerves from the chase, "if he just
leaves every Saturday without saying where he's going or for
how long."

I wondered why the client even hired Frank Streets at all
when the situation appeared obvious: the subject was likely
messing around, and, if not, their relationship was pretty shitty
anyway. I was lucky because I couldn't relate, and I knew it.

But I didn't feel dismissive or judgmental of the client. I
have a soft spot for people who need confirmation of what
seems obvious to others. I think there is art in iteration, in setting off on the same path to find the same proof, every time,
like the philosophy of logic class I took in college where we
had to solve the same problem over and over again each week
to see how many proofs we could find that led to the same conclusion. The mundanity of that work appealed to me, like the
joy I find in repeating a word over and over until it becomes
nonsense—like *cookie cookie cookie cookie* ad infinitum—or
reading something practical aloud—like the instruction manual

for a handheld recorder with added accents on every other dactyl until it sounds like a poem recited at Talk Art in Iowa City.

Maybe the client seeks assurance in asking different questions about her life and discovers herself when the answers are always the same. If this is a ritual of self-actualization, then I am the client.

But I am also suspicious of conclusions. If I find the habits of mind that define me suspect, then I am also the subject.

And I write nothing in stone. I turn conclusions over instead, investigating what others see as self-evident. Even when it seems valueless, inane, or irrational.

I am, finally, the investigator.

I think I know K. She is honest and has the uncanny ability to let knee-jerk responses break down in half-life increments until they dissolve away entirely. She is a patient listener and doesn't burden others with her worries. And, to a fault sometimes, she has the tendency to let people take advantage of her ability to hold volatile emotions in stasis, acting as a container for those close to her to archive their worries. She does share her anxieties with me, but only if I pry.

I believe she is happy with me. I trust that she is, but she must have desires I don't fulfill. She must feel that I am not enough. I prefer to think that she doesn't, that I project a solid shape in her future, but I worry whether my self-involvement ever threatens her. She is so stoic when she says that's not the case when I worry aloud about it, making an emotion that is hers about me, forcing her to keep it hidden with all the others.

And while I am incontinent with my feelings on everything from politics to hangnails, I do keep a part of myself hidden that's made up of all the wild byproducts of my humanness. But repressing those eats away at me. I am aware of bodies in my vicinity and think about sex all the time. I think about killing the neighbor's dog when it barks incessantly every time it's outside, how I would do it with poison stashed in a treat that I casually toss over the fence under cover of night or with a close-range shotgun blast in broad daylight for the brutal drama of it. I fantasize about life without K, about how I would eat and drink and fuck and do whatever, whenever the hell I wanted, and I feel like a failure, like I've already betrayed her even when I haven't.

I might be Freud's ideal subject for his belief that we are animals whose instinctual desires to steal, fuck, and kill are kept in check by our flimsy commitment to social institutions, how our capacity to feel guilt is fundamental to the effectiveness of that order, how our made-up social codes often work without enforcement because we police ourselves with guilt. At least this is true with me: I grope around the space where guilt takes hold, between fantasy and reality, among all the siren songs of wanton desires and the pragmatism of cost–benefit analysis that keeps them in check.

"Some people just wake up and are good. I don't get it. When I wake up in the morning, I have to make the choice to be a good man," my friend Daniel once joked over beers. We were talking about Louis C.K., how he crafts an idea of manhood within his jokes, spotlighting the current of dark fantasies that runs just beneath the surface of his daily routines, the way he teases out a self-serving desire that most men repress, shocking people into laughing at truths they experience but would never admit to. Like his joke about being in the elevator in his apartment building and wishing he could cum like a camel spits, as a defense mechanism, to ward off social pleasantries.

When he broadcasts his private depravity onstage, it is art, but when he lives it, it becomes a problematic truth.

"Tell me about it," I replied to Daniel. "If people knew what I was thinking, like if my thoughts appeared in bubbles above me, I'd end every day alone." Or what if a private investigator was following me, documenting my every move? Could he take enough photographs of me to conclude that I might just be a mediocre husband, father, and writer, fooling everyone I love to believe that I am something better? How would Louis C.K. make that funny?

Frank Streets's cell phone rang. "Why you calling me?" he said. "I'm working!" He held a silent grin for a full minute before he let out a giant chuckle. "I'm in Clarksburg, following a subject. Suspected adulterer. What're you doing?" Frank Streets was talking to his pal Paul Harris, a defense attorney in Wheeling. I would later learn that the majority of the criminal cases Frank Streets worked came from Paul Harris.

When Frank Streets told me about the nature of his work for Paul Harris, it struck me that he might be expected to dig up information that would help get Harris's client off. But Frank Streets assured me he doesn't work like that. "I don't ask him for the details of the case against his client, and I sure don't let any lawyer tell me what to look for. I tell them right away, I'm gonna approach the case like I don't know anything about it, and what I find out is what I find out, and you can decide if you wanna use what I find or not."

He presented himself as an investigator in pursuit of objective facts, a man who sought the truth about the world with an integrity I wished I had. Like he just wakes up and is good.

As Frank Streets and Paul Harris continued with small talk over the phone, the CB chirped occasionally with updates from the white Neon.

"Subject is still inside the garage area."

My blood pressure was elevated from the chase. I tuned out the phone conversation. I took slow, deep breaths and gathered my wits. I looked around. The street wasn't busy. Too early on a Saturday morning. I watched the entrance to Hartland Supply Company across from us. A few dusty and disheveled construction workers shuffled in and out with steaming cups of coffee. Their scraggly beards, hunched backs, and shuffling gaits reminded me of the drunks I see hanging around all hours of the day in downtown Morgantown.

I watched a balding bagel of man in a gray sweatsuit walk slowly out of the store carrying a small plastic bag. He clearly wasn't a construction worker or a contractor. He didn't even look dressed for a weekend DIY project as he moseyed over to a motorized wheelchair parked on the sidewalk. He put his bag in the front basket, mounted the wheelchair, and drove slowly along the sidewalk toward the McDonald's just down the block, bouncing along on the uneven concrete.

"He's been in there a while," the CB chirped. "Seems like too long to just be paying for gas. Over."

As I watched the people move in and out of Hartland, I thought about the Blue Moose, a dive café and diner in Morgantown that serves as many cups of fair-trade coffee to university types as it does two-dollar cans of Stoney's to haggard townies. The Blue Moose attracts an eclectic crowd, and its large windows look out onto one of the busiest intersections in Morgantown. I go there to write but mostly to sit in those windows and watch people. But when I'm sitting there watching the bustle of the city, I don't just passively people-watch like a kid at the mall.

I like to think my people-watching is akin to the scene in *White Men Can't Jump* when Wesley Snipes's character says to Woody Harrelson's character, "You can listen to Jimi, but you can't hear Jimi." I watch people and sometimes never get beneath their surfaces, but I'm always trying to hear Jimi, to understand who they really are and not the idea of who they think they are that they broadcast to the world. I wonder what they see when they watch me sitting in the window, wonder how deep they can mine into me. I am quick to arrange my surfaces to thwart conclusions I'm afraid of.

"The subject's outside. Walking toward his truck."

I find comfort in the fact that the majority of people I see through the Blue Moose windows are as fleeting to me as I am to them. The people I interact with regularly are a different story. Especially the workers behind the counter. They recognize me. We exchange pleasantries. But I am reticent to move into personal terrain with them. I don't even smile at the manager who's always there, whose name I've overheard is Adam, who has a flattop and wire-rim glasses, who almost always wears black jeans and a black Batman T-shirt, who has a tattoo of Groucho Marx on his calf, and who is the father of an eleven-year-old girl named Genevieve. We could chitchat about our tattoos and our children, but like my tattoos, I prefer to keep my personal life private.

"The subject's back inside his truck. Over."

I cast my eyes downward when I'm forced to engage with people on a personal level, like Dani, the woman who pours my coffee in the Blue Moose, who has a lounge bar voice from too many cigarette breaks, who is an artist whose hands shook when one day out of nowhere she showed me photos on her phone of her paintings, still-life flowers and local landscapes in gouache paint that weren't all that memorable, which broke my heart. Her art, her first love, what she cared enough about to be working at a coffee shop to support, to be courageously sharing with me, a person she sees order the same coffee, then sit at the same window and watch the same people and peck away on the same computer at least three times a week for several years but with whom she has never had a meaningful conversation but believes she has something in common with, hopes she does as a fellow artist, and all I can do is smile and nod and politely say, "Cool," my voice not as deep as I want it to sound, and put my earbuds in and quietly wish that her art was better, blush hot that someday she might read something I wrote and think the same about me, that she already knows me enough to understand how that threatens me.

"Subject's pulling out. We're going. Do you copy?"

Thinking back on that moment, I'm not sure if I caught the message the first time it came across the CB. I'm sure I listened to the words, but I didn't hear them. The emotion was wrong. There was no curdled blood, no white knuckles and squealing tires, no sudden clouds of gravel dust as engines shuddered to life in the morning air. It was just a mundane observation, narrated plainly. When I listened to the white Neon repeat the same message over the CB a moment later, I finally heard what was happening. My heart started.

"We're tailing him now. Do you copy do you copy?"

Yes! I copy! But Frank Streets was still engrossed in his phone conversation with Paul Harris. Should I interrupt him? Or wait for him to notice? The subject was on the go, and the CB was deafeningly silent. I imagined the charcoal Tacoma pulling out of the Exxon parking lot; the white Neon watching nonchalantly, the driver twiddling his thumbs deliberately, the passenger holding the CB down and out of sight, unable to shout that the subject was on the move, wondering why the hell Frank Streets wasn't responding and if the CBs were on the fritz again.

"Did they radio?" Frank Streets asked casually as he slipped his cell phone into his breast pocket.

"Yes, I think they said they're going," I croaked. Frank Streets snatched the CB and called the white Neon, barking, "What's going on? You copy?"

"We're going, subject left and is driving west on Pike away from you."

"Don't you lose him," Frank Streets bellowed as we peeled out of our quiet little parking spot, the scene at Hartland jostling away from me like the footage of a camera left recording when trouble arises and there's no other choice than to run. Frank Streets gunned the gas as we exploded through the outskirts of Clarksburg with no way of knowing how far we'd fallen behind the subject. I clutched my seat and scrutinized the road as it unraveled around each curve, desperate for a glimpse of the white Neon.

Frank Streets snatched the CB and wailed hopefully, "You still got him? Where you at!" After only a few seconds, the voice from the Neon replied calmly, "We're on his tail still. We're heading north toward Shinnston. We still got him, but, damn, he's moving fast."

Just as Frank Streets barked back, "Don't get too close, but don't you lose him, you hear?" We came around another bend at high speed and an entrance ramp materialized on our right. Frank Streets jerked the wheel abruptly and pumped the breaks, jolting me into the dashboard as he steered onto the entrance ramp, then swerved aggressively back to the left, tossing me hard into the window as the power steering groaned and we skidded through the loose gravel of the shoulder. We came to a hard stop on the shoulder a few feet from the cement stanchions of the bridge embankment.

"What's that sign say," Frank Streets panted, throwing the Durango into reverse and hitting the gas hard. I tried to regain my balance as he squinted at two signs pointing in opposite directions.

"I think it's that way," he yelped and stomped the gas, throwing me back into the seat as we accelerated under the bridge and followed the road as it doglegged up a steep slope. We roared around the hill and the landscape flattened briefly, allowing a glimpse of at most a quarter mile ahead. No white Neon. Instead, we saw a large coal truck with sooty clouds spewing from both exhausts as it labored up the hill. If our ability to catch the subject had taken a hit when we almost crashed into the bridge embankment, any remaining hope dissipated in a poof of coal dust as we closed in on the truck's bumper.

"Damn!" Frank Streets exclaimed, slamming his fist hard on the steering wheel. "You gotta be kidding me," he muttered. "We gotta get around this truck!" But the double-yellow lines and dangerous curves of the road wouldn't allow it.

Frank Streets grabbed the CB. "You there?" Dead air. He tried again but gave up quickly. He reached for his cell phone and dialed, steering the Durango wildly with one hand.

"How far ahead are you?" he demanded after a few tense seconds. "Damn—we're like four miles behind you! And you're heading right into Shinnston," he muttered with a hint of reticence. Maybe Shinnston connected in some critical way with the backstory he had on the subject. But the emotion was wrong; he would be excited by that confluence. Frank Streets continued, lowering his voice to just above a whisper. "Watch what you say on the phone from here on out."

Frank Streets had told me about the bad blood between himself and the local authorities in Harrison County, where Shinnston is located. It was a case he was investigating for his buddy Paul Harris. Harris was defending Kevin Junkins, a former cop in Shinnston who was accused of stealing drugs from the evidence room and giving it to a local heroin addict to sell for him. After only a few interviews with people around Shinnston, Frank Streets discovered that the corruption ran deeper. From reports he had gathered under oath, numerous cops in the local force were stealing drugs that had been confiscated as evidence and trading them for sexual favors.

Not long after Frank Streets started that case, the Shinnston Sheriff's Office caught wind that he was snooping around. Within a week, several Harrison County sheriff's deputies showed up at Valley View Road trying to confiscate his computers. Frank Streets said they tried intimidating him but he stared them down and they left with a few unimportant files that, he assured me, he allowed them to take. I could tell this was a sensitive situation, and the fact that cops might be looking out for him made me uneasy. I suddenly wasn't sure I wanted my day with Frank Streets to reveal a more exciting story than a middle-aged adulterer with a penchant for leaving for the day unannounced.

As Self-Made Manhood evolved in the late nineteenth and into the early twentieth century, it developed into a collection of achievement badges for straight, white, married men who completed a sequence of Boy Scout-like projects—a good job, a steady paycheck, solid standing in the community, adequate participation as a parent. But if this checklist meant that manhood was something that could be earned and proven, then it was also something that must be maintained at the risk of being lost.

I was never a Boy Scout, but I was a Cub Scout for one year in elementary school. I don't remember much of what we did at our den meetings, but I do remember the pinewood derby and the racecar the size of a chalkboard eraser my dad helped me build. We carved and sanded it, painted it red, applied decal numbers to the hood, and glued the torso of an action figure into the cockpit.

My memory of the race itself is of a throng of fathers teaching sons how to yell for their little cars to roll fast down a ramp in a musty church basement. My car didn't win the race, but someone at the event handed me a plastic sleeve the size of a playing card that had a badge with an image of a bear embroidered on it. The importance of the event wasn't in winning or losing the race but in earning the right to announce my participation in this tradition of American boyhood to other fathers and sons who had earned the same badge.

I admired the physical construction of my badge—the high-gloss thread and textured relief of the embroidery—but I wasn't into the effort it would take to earn more, so I quit Cub Scouts and never looked back.

Independent of my youthful fetish for textiles, Kimmel would argue that when manhood became a badge-earning activity and a man's status could not only be observed but measured, the landscape of masculinity had shifted for the Self-Made Man, and the sure footing of his identity would forever be changed. A fear of emasculation entered the psyche of men, and "for the first time in American history," Kimmel writes, "young men experienced 'identity crises.'"

I discovered the truth about myself on my thirtieth birthday. It was just before eleven o'clock in the morning with the sun not shining and a look of hard wet rain in the cold air of the Appalachian foothills that surround Morgantown. I was wearing sweatpants and a tie-dyed T-shirt. I was staring at my blank computer screen, drinking coffee, unshaven, and mildly hungover. I had been dreading this birthday for a year. Or really, I had been trying to convince myself I wasn't dreading this birthday for at least two years, as if I hadn't built it up to be the commencement of my middle age with nothing to show for it.

I was also unable to deny that my desire to be a writer was out of sync with the settled and mundane life I had been living since K and I got married and moved to West Virginia. We had been living in Morgantown for two years, having moved there when she was offered a position as an assistant professor of political science at West Virginia University. For one of us to have a real job with real money was just too good to be true, so we moved, even though I still had a year left in my MFA program and a thesis I needed to write to complete my degree.

As a result, I spent my first year living in West Virginia as an adjunct composition instructor, my time divided between teaching four courses, writing alone in the Blue Moose, and traveling back to Iowa City to confirm that my thesis committee didn't get off on the conceptual highfalutinness of my project as much as I did. Not that I blame them. I took an anthology of "the best" nonfiction and inserted myself into it through the use of footnotes. It was a take on Nabokov's *Pale Fire* where I was Kinbote and the other essayists were my John Shade. I believed I was creating a critique of the way we exploit other people's stories to help us craft our own, and in doing so, exact the versions of ourselves we want to be true. I thought by critiquing that act through my own participation in it I might conjure a more sincere and authentic self-portrait than I could in any other form of writing or art.

I wanted to use myself as a tool to comment on the self-obsessed culture of memoir I observed around me, make myself into a literary equivalent of Andy Warhol, my all-time artist-hero whose public persona as the chic and vapid guru of the New York art scene embodied the celebrity culture of the sixties as much as any glamorous portrait of Marilyn, Elvis, or Mao he ever silkscreened. His identity was his magnum opus. And even if his identity-based brand of conceptual art had enough theory behind it to fill a dozen art-history dissertations, his version of pop art was still playful and just plain old fun if that's all you wanted from it.

But my thesis wasn't much fun at all, and my theory failed miserably. It revealed nothing about writing, nothing about identity, and certainly nothing sincere or authentic about me. If Warhol loosened a cultural knot in a room filled with silver balloons, I would've taken the same balloons and inundated their surfaces with unintended proclamations of the importance of my perspective that whooshed the fun right out them, then desperately tried to recapture it with convoluted explanations to anyone within earshot of the meaning they should be getting from my dreadfully unfun balloons.

I've come to accept that I'm more inclined to make a knot than I am to untie one. And I could spend some time turning that over and over here on the page, formulating a theory of how that act in itself is important—but that would just be more of me knotting as a way to argue my perspective is important. The more I inserted myself into the sincere and authentic and earnest lives that germinate in other writers' words, the more I encountered a central problem with my thesis: how could I have hoped to develop a sincere self-portrait by exploiting the stories of other people's lives? My thesis was indebted to a practice of colonialism, and any portrait of me that could ever have emerged was colored by my naive participation in a tradition of white, patriarchal privilege.

And a few months after my thirtieth birthday, after the year-deep layer of dust on my MFA degree had revealed the hard truth that the degree does not the writer make, K and I were sitting in traffic in Morgantown on our way to Walmart. I was probably slouching in the passenger seat, sulking like an adolescent not getting his way. It was then that I saw a shabby storefront sign advertising BOB CLAY INVESTIGATIONS and had an idea: I would hire Bob Clay to follow me around for a day and write a report concluding what he could about me. Then, I could write about the self-consciousness of being investigated and react to Bob Clay's report to see what I learned about myself. I might actually reveal something authentic about myself if I let someone evaluate me outside of my control. Bingo! It would be the opposite of my unfun thesis, a mashup of two projects by Sophie Calle, one of my other all-time artist-heroes, who in one work had herself evaluated by a psychologist and then published the report, and in another hired a private investigator to follow her around and take pictures of her going about her daily routine. And that's what I would do: I would hire Bob Clay to follow me around, document my mundane routines, and then conclude what he could about my character. If I couldn't just reveal myself directly, sincerely, honestly, my fears, my deficiencies, my self-interest on my own, maybe a private i's report would be the crutch I needed. Maybe high art wasn't my bag, and a detective story was the hook I needed.

A few weeks later, after I had spent more than enough time googling his name, scouring his website, and writing down the names of other local PIs he probably competed with for clients, I decided to take a closer look at Bob Clay's office. I needed the fresh air, anyway. I grabbed a crumpled pair of jeans off the floor, threw on a jacket, and hoofed it ten minutes to downtown Morgantown. Bob Clay Investigations is in a red brick building where the Westover Bridge crosses the Monongahela River and intersects with Don Knotts Boulevard. Don Knotts is the most famous native of Morgantown, and his memory is fittingly honored with one of the busiest intersections in the city. I walked by Bob Clay's office to take a look at the shingle hanging above the entrance. It looked like flimsy composite plastic, and it was smudged with grime from years of swaying amidst the parade of coal trucks that belch along the boulevard. BOB CLAY INVESTIGATIONS was printed largely in a faded shade of blue along the top, with a phone number and a list of a few services rendered beneath it. I typed the number into my phone but didn't call. I jammed my phone in my pocket and walked across the street to get a better look at the place. No people entering or leaving. No lights on. The shudders were drawn in all the windows. No flutter of blinds. It was just another run-down two-story office building in Morgantown. The whole scene had the look of a picture frame with a thick layer of dust settled on it.

As I trudged home, I pulled my phone out of my pocket and looked at the number I'd typed in. I pressed call.

"Hello?" the brusque male voice that answered seemed unsurprised I was calling. I swallowed hard.

"Hello, is this Bob Clay?" I squawked.

"Yes, it is," the voice responded impatiently.

I cleared my throat and tried to sound professional, puffing up with a deep breath and throwing my shoulders back. "Hi, hello, this is Stephen J. West. I'm a, a writer, and I'm calling because I'm hoping that I could talk to you about your experiences as a private investigator." I figured I would come off as a creep if I admitted right away that I wanted him to follow me around. My plan was to talk to him for a while, feel him out, then convince him I wasn't totally depraved.

"Well, I'm 90 percent retired at this point," Bob Clay responded. "Mostly what I do now is polygraphing. So." This made sense, his office building looked 90 percent retired, too. I suspected the conversation was over, but I pressed him anyway.

"Oh, wow, okay. But I still think it might be useful if I could talk to you about your past work, you know, what you've experienced over the course of your career," I said and tortured my lip.

"I don't really do what you're interested in," he stated with finality. He wasn't messing around; this was a professional brush off. My shoulders slumped as the air whooshed out of me like a balloon. But magically, Bob Clay continued. "You know, my associate Frank Streets down in Barbour County, he's a former sheriff's deputy. He still does a lot of surveillance and the kind of stuff you're into." I was so close to bursting that I missed the poignant irony of Bob Clay's analysis of the "kind of stuff" I was "into," oblivious to how his comment reduced me to a "writer type," nor how accurate that was. I could care less. I had another lead.

"Frank Streets might talk to you," Bob Clay concluded. "I can give you his number."

"Okay, that would be great," I replied eagerly. I nervously wrote down Frank Streets's number and mustered one last appeal to Bob Clay. I'd spent too much time privately obsessing over him to have it all go up like a cloud of coal smoke. "And like I said, I'm interested in researching lots of things about private investigation, so if it turns out I need to speak with someone about lie detector tests, would you be willing to chat with me about that in the future?"

"Why don't you give Frank Streets a call and, you know, we'll see."

I often need confirmation for how my behaviors are interpreted by others when, really, they should be self-evident. It should be self-evident that I annoy K by repeatedly asking her if I annoy her when I ask if something is wrong for no reason other than to hear her say "No, Steve, nothing is wrong"; it should be self-evident that my hair is just too contradictorily thick and receding to look good styled any other way than short, no matter how much I want to have long, flowing hair once before I die; it should be self-evident that I apologize too much, assuming that I'm somehow responsible for every failure in my vicinity.

Even if I'm unable to see myself objectively, there isn't a scenario where I wouldn't want to know the truth. As much as I close myself off from people like Adam and Dani at the Blue Moose and every other Adam and Dani in my life, I am far more open with K.

I like to believe that K and I both value the open dialogue we have about our feelings—even if that can veer toward annoyance when I ask her if everything's okay and am too impatient to listen to the answer, getting distracted by a glimpse of my weird swatch of hair in the reflection of a storefront window, wondering if it's again time to give up on growing it out. But I don't need perpetual revelation (ironic, I know, vis-à-vis the current context). I'm not one of those compulsive sharers who will hold you hostage to whatever issues they're dealing with on any given day, even if you just met them. You know the brand I'm talking about: the one who dials you in for a long story when you can't escape—in the line at the post office, at a bar when it's busy enough that you have to sit next to someone you don't know but not busy enough that you can just ignore them entirely, or when you bum a cigarette and really just want to smoke the cigarette, not find a new best friend. The kind of personal revelation that develops within those encounters feels like the fliers that lie unacknowledged on my porch for days, fluttering into irrelevance when I open my screen door, no matter how thoughtfully someone tucked them in.

There is this one young woman who regularly frequents the Blue Moose. She's a textbook example of the personality type whose self-revelation, if it were akin to an airport terror warning, would never drop below ORANGE. I'd guess she's in her mid-twenties, skinny, maybe even pretty as a first impression. But she is arrestingly self-conscious. She makes eye contact with everyone. Like she is looking for someone to share every moment with, not just those that have meaning. And she talks nonstop about herself. No matter who she sits with she narrates anecdote after anecdote aloud, about what happened with this guy at the bar, about what happened afterward, about what happened the next morning, about how he hasn't called her in days, about how she ran into him at the bar the next week, about how he ignored her at first but by the end of the night was paying attention to her again. Life relived out loud, with a quivering lower lip, with the most earnest melodrama, while the person she sits with looks down repeatedly and doesn't say much. Sometimes she's alone, but that doesn't impact the volume of her self-revelation; if she isn't broadcasting her life to the Blue Moose in an hour-long phone call, she's pouting at her computer screen and wearing giant headphones with the volume cranked so high that the tinny racket she's listening to must be unbearable. Like the dude who blasts music from his car as it slowly rolls down the street, his arm dangling deliberately from the open window, she imagines we are listening along with her, that we can feel the analogy the song makes to whatever drama is unfolding in her mind. I understand how she could be just impulsively self-centered, and her stories and music could be just for her—not meant to be analyzed and resolved, just aired publicly—as if something important is conjured in the act of repeatedly reflecting on one's mundane life aloud that I am uncomfortable doing myself, fearful of how it necessarily opens me up for judgment.

And yet I do.

I've concluded that all the music she plays, like all the stories she tells, all of it is for you and me; all of it is a plea for any of us to just know her, to care a little bit about her. It's a matter of survival.

The irony is that while she is one of the more obnoxious people I see at the Blue Moose, she is also my favorite. I admire her obsessive earnestness and feel for the desperate way she clings to fleeting eye contact. I apologize to her in my mind for never sitting down with her to just listen like she needs someone to, to tell her how I admire how she relentlessly opens herself up for everyone's judgment, how I admire her fearlessness.

Frank Streets clutched the CB handset to his massive chest and tilted his head down slightly to speak.

"I'm pulling in up ahead here," he said to his other car as we approached Clarksburg, the highway winding across the valley below us with its hit list of exit-ramp gas stations and chain restaurants standing witness to the steady flow of truck traffic. We turned into the Bob Evans parking lot.

He cut the engine and picked up his cell phone. "I guess I better call the client," he groaned.

"Hello, this is Frank Streets," he declared, then continued before the client could air even a trivial greeting in response. "Let me ask you something: is there any chance he knew he was being followed?" No way! I answered to myself, scrobbling my memory of "the chase" for a clue that the subject was suspicious of us on his tail, but there was nothing; he wasn't; we just lost him.

Frank Streets furrowed his brow into a kind of confidence. "Well, he left just like you said he would, and we followed him into Clarksburg to an Exxon Station. He went into the Exxon, and I was parked a little ways away. So my other car followed him out of the Exxon when he left, heading north on 19 and 20 toward Shinnston." The timbre of his voice went up, as if it was a revealing detail. "So, my other car is tailing him, and he's hauling ass—I mean, he's hauling, doing over seventy, and my car's doing everything they can just to keep up with him. There's a car in between them, see, and when they get into Shinnston—you know the light just past the McDonald's and the state police headquarters there? Well, he runs clear through a red light!" Frank Streets paused theatrically, his eyes widening, clearly pleased with how the client was reacting to his falsified report of her husband's reported getaway. "That tells me he's making damn sure he can't be followed, is what it is—he's making damn sure."

A therapist and a PI may share in their desire to seek solutions for the people they work for, but after listening to the tale Frank Streets crafted for the client, I sensed that a PI and a writer aren't so different in their desire to get what they want.

After a brief conversation that included Frank Streets sharing his plan to stake out the subject next weekend, he slipped his cell phone into his breast pocket. "Well, that went better than I thought," he turned to me and said with relief. "Client said he came over here to Shinnston last week, that he was looking at property."

My eyes focused on the sudden navy blue of the dashboard. "What, here in Shinnston? Looking to buy property? Is she not looking at it with him?" I asked eagerly, my voice clanging with desperation that revealed my hope that there was still more for us to investigate.

"Nope, she found some paperwork in his briefcase. Something about a little log cabin up around here that he was looking at."

"And she didn't say anything to him?"

"Nope, she just looked at it and left it in the briefcase, and the next day it was gone." First the subject regularly leaves for hours at a time with no explanation, then he buys a crotch rocket in cash, then has a brown belt in karate, and now he's purchasing a log cabin forty-five minutes from his home without mentioning it to his wife. I wondered again why we needed to follow this guy at all. His infidelity seemed obvious to me.

As we stepped out into the Bob Evans parking lot, Frank Streets looked around in mock suspicion.

"You just don't know where you'll see him," he whispered. "You just never know. He may show up here." As I laughed at the idea of finding the subject at Bob Evans, the white Neon pulled into a spot near us. Frank Streets and I got out and moseyed over to greet the investigators in his other car for the first time.

"Stephen, this is Nick. I call him Half-Unit. And this is my daughter Joanne."

"Nice to meet you," I said in my best professional writer voice, something I decided should be between engaging and distant. Joanne was wearing baggy blue jeans and a gray hooded sweatshirt, and her blond hair was knotted up in a messy ponytail. She was like a smaller version of Frank Streets, from the stocky physique to the gleaming eyes and ready smile that looked like it was always itching for banter.

Half-Unit was slouched with his hands in his jean's pockets. He was thin, wearing a flannel shirt and Red Wing construction boots, and I could just see his frown and downcast eyes beneath his soiled white baseball cap. I shook Joanne's and then Half-Unit's hands firmly, noting that Joanne's voice was deeper than my own.

"You don't think that's him," Frank Streets gasped and squatted down slightly, freezing in place as we made our way through the dining area. He stood transfixed, still as a hunter happening upon fresh tracks, his intensity surreal amid the din of tableware on cheap ceramic and dulcet melody of blue-eyed soul filtering from the overhead speakers. His eyes were glued on the parking lot, visible through the venetian blinds behind a row of booths across from us. Joanne took the same posture and looked where he was pointing, both bending over at the waist and jerking their heads back and forth in response to the blinds. Half-Unit trudged behind, his hands still jammed in his pockets as he cast a casual look toward the window. I stole a look, too, and saw row upon row of pickup truck after pickup truck.

"It's the same color and everything," Frank Streets said. "But that's not it. His plate is NEH something. That's not it."

Frank Streets and Joanne both straightened up and scanned the dining area as we resumed nonchalance on the way to our booth. The four of us slid into place, Half-Unit and Joanne on one side, Frank Streets and me on the other. The hostess left without making eye contact with any of us.

"What am I going to get," Frank Streets chirped excitedly as he snatched up the glossy menu. "I don't know if I want breakfast or lunch." He squinted at the hypercolor pictures of sandwiches draped with glistening meats. "Somebody make a choice here."

"I'm doing grilled cheese," I said and placed my menu down with an authority I hoped would cover my worry that grilled cheese was a decidedly unmanly selection. K and I had recently committed to an entirely plant-based diet, but I figured she would agree that ordering grilled cheese was a better move than ordering a salad and raising serious concern over just what the fuck I was trying to pull.

"You're doing grilled cheese," Frank Streets repeated with a touch of wonder and raised his eyebrows, as if my choice was odd in a cutesy way like someone from Europe taking a break for "tea," and actually drinking tea.

"I'm going lunch," I said gruffly, trying to suggest where grilled cheese might be viewed on the spectrum of manly meals.

"I better look at lunch, too," Frank Streets replied and flipped through the menu. "Look at that smokehouse burger platter," he catcalled. "Oh my god, I may have to get that."

"It looks good," I lied, trying to earn my way back into the table's cultural comfort zone.

The waitress stomped back up to us, and I led off by ordering my grilled cheese, speaking quickly to minimize its wimpiness. Joanne ordered hotcakes, and Half-Unit ordered a chicken potpie. Then came Frank Streets's turn.

"Give me this cheddar baked-potato soup," he began.

"Cup or bowl," the waitress asked drolly.

Frank Streets paused, weighing the gravity of the decision. "Bowl," he said, confirming with a nod. "Then give me the smokehouse chicken sandwich." He went lunch. "Also give me a side order of sausage links," he added impulsively, veering back into breakfast. "And a side order of bacon. Now that chicken sandwich, it comes with bacon, right?" I chuckled uncomfortably, then bit my lip. No one else laughed; there was nothing funny about his question.

Eventually our food was delivered, and I tried to look barrel-chested as I took aggressive bites of my grilled cheese, making sure to eat all the crusts. Just after a thorough discussion of the size of the chicken chunks in Half-Unit's potpie, Joanne looked at me.

"What's your wife think of this," she asked with a smirk. Her eyes drilled into mine, smirkless.

"She's fine, I think," I laughed and looked down, "although I don't think I'll tell her about the high-speed chase. Maybe I'll tell her I got to carry a gun," I added jokingly. "But she might not find that so funny. We have a nine-month-old at home, so she'll want me to stay safe."

"We have lots of youngsters," Joanne chirped, elbowing Half-Unit, indicating they were a couple. "I have a four-year-old, a three-year-old, a two-year-old, and a two-month-old."

"Wow, that's a big family," I said, unable to hide my surprise. My best guess was that Joanne was in her mid-twenties. I was in my early thirties, having dragged my feet to have even one kid. Most of my friends were in their mid-thirties and still didn't have kids. Many weren't even married. They were busy living in cities like New York and Chicago and L.A., pursuing their careers as writers and artists, finding success I was envious of, and making enough money to live lives of adventure with prospects that seemed like pipe dreams compared to the turn toward middle-class anonymity my life had taken since moving to West Virginia. I followed their lives with burning envy, tuning into the images of glamor and culture and accomplishment they posted on social media. I was jealous of their freedom from family responsibility, their seeming ability to invest in whatever they wanted to at any moment of the day.

"So, what are you writing about?" Joanne's eyes needled me. I choked on a potato chip.

Kimmel shows that Self-Made American Men have been defined by a continued history of fear, frustration, and failure, "and many of our actions on both the public and private stages," Kimmel surmises, "have been efforts to ward off these demons, to silence these fears." He argues that a "crisis moment" like the one facing traditional American Masculinity will often lead to projects of critical self-investigation.

Like writing a book that investigates manhood, for example. Why don't you dig into that.

Kimmel writes, "we tend to search for the timeless and eternal during moments of crisis, those points of transition when the old definitions no longer work and the new definitions are yet to be firmly established." And writing that book about American manhood is itself a social phenomenon, a marker of an era where gender has become a conscious and contentious forum.

In a period like our own.

While his project might be deemed as exclusionary in its focus on the white American man—yet another, tired example of attention being lavished on the patriarchal and racial privilege of this identity—at the very least, it is a book trying to answer a feminist call to men to acknowledge the privileges they are granted by birthright. "We continue to treat our male military, political, scientific, or literary figures as if their gender, their masculinity had nothing to do with their military exploits, policy decisions, scientific experiments, or writing styles and subjects. We must make gender visible to men," he argues.

What do I know?

"Well, I'm a professor, in English," I swallowed, intentionally leaving out "adjunct" to try to gain some credibility, but it landed with a snobby thud as I pushed the last of my crusts of my grilled cheese to the side of my plate. "I'm writing about, well, I'm just starting to write a book," I sniffled and swallowed. "I'm interested in private investigations, in getting to know what PIs go through to get to the bottom of things. It's about people—and writing. And my life. I'm not really sure what it's about," I squawked. "I'm just trying to figure it out, too," I chuckled and buried my face in my soda. I couldn't bear to look at them, to make eye contact and see just what conclusions they had drawn about me.

A few minutes passed while Frank Streets and Joanne shared bits of observations and reactions to the morning's events, the narrative emerging in a chaotic gestalt of serious concerns and silly responses. Half-Unit remained silent, pressed into the booth.

"So, what else do you do?" Frank Streets asked, turning toward me.

"You mean besides write?" I sipped my soda coolly and held impossibly still.

"Yeah, like hobbies." He knew I didn't hunt, and coming from a man with a den that would make a Cabela's catalogue jealous, he was honestly curious just what I did with my spare time.

"I like camping and hiking," I said, figuring that might pass as acceptable.

Frank Streets chewed a piece of bacon contemplatively. "Have you ever seen anything you can't explain while you're out there in the woods?" I was caught off guard. I felt like Miss West Virginia fielding a curveball question in the interview phase of my pageant.

"When I'm camping? Or just in general?" I replied, not sure what he was after.

"Do you believe in ghosts?" Frank Streets asked with a straight face.

"I knew he was getting there. I knew it, I knew it!" Joanne blurted with a wide smile and thrust herself backward in the booth.

"Is this like a trap or something?" I joked.

She continued, "No, he's seriously all about these TV shows. *Ghost Hunters*, you know, paranormal stuff, everything like that."

Frank Streets ignored his daughter's outburst and responded quickly to his own question, "I'm not gonna say I don't believe in them, but I'm gonna say at this point, I've never seen nothing I can't explain. So for me to say I believe in them, I'm gonna have to see it."

"Yeah. I dunno," I answered thoughtfully. I believe some of the stories don't have good answers, but I don't know if I'm like, 'Oh yeah, there's definitely something going on.'"

"That's what I'm getting at, exactly," Frank Streets pounded the table emphatically.

"I went and spent 700 dollars. I've got boxes I can show you, filled with ghost-hunting stuff. I've got all the gadgets."

"You've got 700 dollars' worth of ghost-hunting equipment?" I couldn't hide my surprise.

"I'll show it to you sometime. Recorder, laser lights, K2 meters, ghost box, voice recorder, spirit box, EMF. I've played with the stuff everywhere. I ticked my wife off. I've got all these old masks I bought from Africa, thirty-six of them in a box for 400 bucks. I'm gonna hang them all upstairs. She wanted me to get rid of them because she said they're haunted. After I bought them, I had them all laid out, and I took the K2 meter and ran it across all of them and there was nothing. 'See I told you,' she said. Well, she's got her dad in an urn up there, so I said, 'Okay, let's check your dad out, see if he's doing anything.'" He grinned at Joanne and she shook her head. "It didn't pick up anything," he added with disappointment. "But we are going to the Moundsville penitentiary to try my gadgets out," he said happily.

"When?" my mind immediately started strategizing how I could invite myself along. "If you need another person, count me in." I imagined a night in a haunted house with Frank Streets and $700 worth of ghost-hunting equipment would definitely be worth my time.

"I will. I'll let you know. A couple of the girls I want to come with us are too freaked out." He tilted his head and squinted at me, like he was wondering if I was also too freaked out. "I don't believe in any of this. But," he paused, leaning in close to me. "There's always a but," he whispered like a secret he was sharing only with me.

On the drive back to Morgantown, I scrutinized my rearview mirror for vehicles weaving through traffic the perfect distance behind me. I exhaled more than I breathed in, and my thoughts swirled like a Pollock painting.

A father–daughter private-investigation team tearing through the hillbilly hinterland on the tail of an adulterer, with a terrified writer along for the ride: the premise was a better fit for a reality show than for a work of art. I felt exhilarated, like I'd just discovered something important, but the buzz dissipated as I reflected upon the glimpses into the people's lives I'd just experienced. As much as it was a thrill to play the role of Frank Streets's sidekick, laughing at his jokes and listening wide-eyed to his ghost stories, I also felt sobered by his self-assuredness. I felt a rush that we'd hid in broad daylight from the local cops who were out to get Frank Streets, but it was quickly leveled by the whiff of fear the people in Shinnston must feel every time they get pulled over on a backroad, hoping the police answer to an authority other than their personal desires. It made my anxiety about my identity even more pathetic.

Frank Streets, his daughter Joanne, Half-Unit, even the client and her husband: it would be so simple to reduce them to archetypes readers would understand, so easy to use them as devices to help perform a drama in which I played the starring role. But they are real and important and dynamic and worth so much more than a cheap canvas upon which I might paint a portrait of myself. And, really, who needs my self-portrait? Without them as props, my story is not worth writing about beyond its easy proof of Tocqueville's theory that "Nothing conceivable is so petty, so insipid, so crowded with paltry interests—in one word, so anti-poetic—as the life of a man in the United States." I wrung the steering wheel like an uptight masseur, the stiff rubber popping into place with the rhythm of my grip.

I could try and do something selfless, to help others somehow, but I've never been that brave. I could quit writing and go back to school to be a social worker; I could run for a local political office and try to be a good servant, work my ass off to improve the lives of people in need; I could volunteer at a homeless shelter or a Boys & Girls Club for a few hours a week; hell, I could invest myself in my teaching, my students, not think being an adjunct is beneath me like I'd earned something better when I hadn't, not view my job as a hoop to jump through just to get back to what matters: finding the du jour subject to chase in pursuit of art. I mean, what the fuck is the point in that? Who does that help? But it suits me; I'm only ever beholden to my personal desires, no better than an adulterer. I felt like I had more in common with the decrepit backroads, ramshackle storefronts, and slumping characters in West Virginia than I ever had before. I felt sad and at home in that sadness.

It has become an annual tradition that the Gallup–Healthways Well-Being Index awards West Virginia the conspicuous honor of being the saddest and most stressed state in the nation, where residents are more apt to say they are "stressed," "angry," "sad," or "worried" than anywhere else in the United States. If these results aren't enough to make a person wary of how they might feel living there, West Virginia has the dubious distinction of earning top honors for percentage of adults who smoke, are obese, have adult diabetes, are the least educated (with less than 20 percent of residents holding a bachelor's degree or higher), and who earn the lowest median household income in the nation.

While Morgantown isn't a large enough metropolitan area to be ranked on its own, the district in which it is surveyed regularly scores in the last quintile of the category "life evaluation," and in the middle quintile of "emotional health."

In other words, people in Morgantown feel so-so about their shitty lives. I could relate, although I think a more realistic portrait of my feelings while living in West Virginia would be that I felt shitty about my so-so life.

West Virginia wasn't the place K and I had dreamed of moving to, and our conversations with friends in more desirable locales went something like this: It's a job! It's not like we're moving there for good. It's just the first stop along the way. Hey! It's a job. Even between ourselves, we'd rationalized the decision to move to West Virginia, viewing it as an exotic place we'd live for a short time. It would be like a study abroad: we'd stay just long enough to sample the pepperoni rolls and bluegrass music, apply for jobs in other places where we'd rather live, and leave before our distinctly non-Appalachian identities were irreparably changed. One of us would get a job and we'd be moving on, probably sooner than later. Certainly before either of us started to talk like them. That was the plan.

But the academic job market is competitive. I knew I had basically a 0 percent chance to land any of the creative-writing jobs I applied for, but K's career had real promise; she was publishing her research and being awarded large grants, but even she wasn't finding any luck with the applications she regularly sent out. Not even a whiff of an interview.

I was nervous it might not be so easy to move, and the more I worried about being stuck, the more I blamed West Virginia for everything from my friends and family not visiting more often to not being able to find a store that carried the craft beer that I liked to my stalled aspirations to be a writer.

It hadn't always been that way.

When K and I left Iowa City for Morgantown, we were starry eyed, as young people in love in their mid-twenties are when they move somewhere together for the first time. So what if it was Morgantown and not New York or Chicago or L.A.—it was ours, and while K defended her dissertation, my grad-school buddies Shawn and Scott helped me pack our moving truck. I remember being giddy at the thought of moving to a place on the outskirts of the coastal cultural radar.

It wasn't unfamiliar to me, after all; I'd grown up in Livonia, New York, a small town in Livingston County, about thirty miles south of Rochester. Western New York is the state's take on the Midwest, the hinterland to people who thought only of New York City when I would say I was from New York, not imagining that the Big Apple was twice as far away from me as Pittsburgh, Cleveland, or even Toronto. Agriculture is the leading industry in Livingston County, and I grew up being referred to as a *hick* and a *bumpkin* by kids from Rochester. I didn't grow up on a farm, but it still burned me up every time I heard it, because they were right; I grew up in a place cable television didn't reach, amid stretches of cornfields and slumping barns. There were no parks or playgrounds near my house; I swung on barn ropes and crawled through drainage pipes; I hiked through fields and creeks, through "Uncle Bill's Junkyard," a hillside field less than a mile from my house that was covered with the flaking carcasses of rusted mid-century tractors, with blackberries, sweet peas, and Queen Anne's lace blooming around their oxidized frames. I rode busses to school with the smell of fresh manure rising from the aisle.

But I wasn't a hick. I was privileged for Livingston County, considered rich by my classmates because my parents were teachers with steady incomes and my father drove a used Corvette. I was stung by how others viewed me, not wanting to be a hick from one perspective, not wanting to be rich and privileged from another, afraid both were accurate. I loathed the limits that being from a rural place seemed to pose, and as I snuck around in old barns and rode my bike on backroads among the sizzle of summer crickets, I daydreamed of moving to somewhere glamorous and romantic like New York City.

When we moved to West Virginia, I viewed it as a chance to redeem my juvenile cynicism of the rural and backwater as being culturally defunct, to prove to myself that the city does not make the man. K and I would craft West Virginia in our image, make it alternative and intellectual and artsy, a haven from the values of a middle-class and suburban lifestyle that we imagined ourselves against. Even a young Andrew Warhol grew up just seventy miles north in the Polish working-class slums of Pittsburgh, and I was convinced I'd find the same magical artistic inspiration as he did once upon a time. And who knows? Maybe we'd even stick in West Virginia, settle into a humble mountainside cabin overlooking our own private Walden Pond, where I could write meditative essays on how all of existence is held in a goose honk, raise goats and hens, make craft cheeses and sell them at a local farmers market, unleashing the heroic artisan within.

My spirit soared with optimism, and I felt creative and

charismatic and smart and handsome enough to tailor West Virginia to my identity as a writer and an artist with something—EVERYTHING!—to say. I must have felt that way. Why would I have gunned the throttle and rocketed my motorcycle up our moving truck's ramp without a wobble if I was fearful of the future?

But the world tilted about nine hours later as I crossed the Ohio River and careened through Wheeling, looking in my side mirror for K driving our rusty Accord, wondering if she felt the wheel wobble out of control as we hurdled above the crosshatch of steel bridges and squat red brick buildings clumped among the muscled landscape.

It tilted again as we exited I-79 into Morgantown, when I misjudged the severe incline of the ramp and almost rolled the moving truck, skidding to a stop in a stretch of wet grass a few feet from the guardrail and a long, long way down.

It tilted for good when I pulled our moving truck up to the front door of the apartment we'd rented along the top of Grand Street, the steep thoroughfare that cuts through South Park, the neighborhood where many university types lived (read: the people most like us in the entire state of West Virginia). I hopped out and nearly fell, having to grab the side of the truck to steady myself. Sure, we were only ten hours removed from the flatness of the Midwest, but the severe incline of the street we now called home prompted the question: how do you keep your spirit soaring when you begin to believe that the nature of a place pulls you down?

I eyed the doors to the bed of the moving truck. The hill must have been a shade under a 45-degree angle. I thought warily of my motorcycle hidden behind the mass of boxes and furniture, of K's and my entire existence suddenly cutting loose and tumbling down the hill until it crashed in a heap at the bottom of Decker's Creek about a half mile below us.

We unpacked our moving truck, and nothing tumbled down the hill that day. But as K and I looked at each other the moment I lifted the latch and the doors swung open, I was fearful of the future for the first time in our young relationship, the way my life was tilting away from me and my desires and toward the responsibility required by living with and for someone else.

"I'm seeing flashes," K said as if she wasn't quite sure she believed it, wiping her right eye slowly with her index finger. We were sitting on the couch watching a hockey game. It was late October, just three months having passed since we unpacked our moving truck.

"Weird," I responded. Or I didn't respond at all, I can't remember because K didn't make a big deal of it. I assumed it was the same as when I say my ears are ringing.

"I'm still seeing flashes," she said again the next day when we were eating dinner at the beautiful oak dining table we'd bought earlier that day at a flea market in the outskirts of Morgantown. We'd tied it to the top of our Accord with twine, worried it might slide off as we drove up to our apartment on Grand Street. It was the only thing we'd purchased, though I'd considered buying the goat that was jammed in a pet carrier until I saw the thick green mucus oozing from its nose, the man assuring me it just had a little cold.

"Does it hurt?" I asked, munching my salad.

"No. It's just so strange. It's like, I see a streak of light in the same exact spot. Over and over again—it's exactly the same every time."

"Like seeing stars? I see stars sometimes if I hit my head or stand up too fast. They kind of swirl around from the edges of my vision, bursting rapidly at first then kind of fading away. Like that?"

She shook her head slowly, still so deep in the experience of the flashes that she couldn't even shoot me a condescending look.

I have no idea why I didn't ask her more about it then. Why

I didn't ask her how long she had been seeing flashes. Why I didn't just fucking google "flashes in eye" or "why does someone see flashes in eye" or "what to do for flashes in eye." I just shrugged it off, not thinking it could be anything severe. Hey, we were in our twenties. What could possibly go wrong?

Not that I blame West Virginia for K's having detached retinas in her mid-twenties—not an uncommon medical event, but nearly unheard of at such a young age—first in her right eye, then again a year later in her left eye. That's on her having the rare distinction of being both extremely myopic and having oblong shaped eyes that lend themselves to retinal tears.

But I do blame West Virginia for the botched surgery by her cavalier young doctor that left her right eye with a damaged nerve and a field of vision that's in permanent twilight, how he patted her on the shoulder and said with a smile, "bad things happen to good people."

I blame West Virginia for the lawyer who told us we had no case for a malpractice suit, saying, "There's just some things you don't do local in West Virginia."

"We need to perform a vitrectomy, sucking out the vitreous gel in her eye and replace the fluid with a gas bubble," said another surgeon at the West Virginia University Eye Institute without glancing at her file, when a year later K's retina detached in her left eye, even after we explained it was that same procedure that damaged her optic nerve and left her right eye permanently blind.

"Isn't there another way?" K whimpered. "Given what happened last time?"

"No. It's how we do it here," the surgeon said without looking up once.

"We can seal off the tear with noninvasive laser," said the specialist at Will's Eye in Philadelphia after listening closely to K's story, after we drove six hours seeking help from the world beyond West Virginia.

Ten minutes later, the laser procedure was done, and at the time I am writing this, K can still see with her left eye using a corrective lens.

I am reticent to share the emotional quotients of K's vision loss because I can only interpret it through the prism of my experience, what she shared, and how I feel. How this trauma impacted her perspective on who she is and the world she now moves through, how she makes sense of it—the assumptions it would require I make for her experience, the way the gravity of my subjectivity would bend it toward a revelation of my identity, makes it a story I don't feel I have the privilege to tell. "Que sais-je?" Montaigne would ask. What do I know? And my answer is that I don't know what it's like to lose my vision. I can't know the many dimensions of that, and an attempt to portray it would be like a flat-Earther explaining where the sun goes after sunset.

What I do know is that K's vision was the moment I committed myself to her more than I ever had before. I had to prioritize her needs over my own every day, sacrificing myself to help her manage her disability. From the countless hours spent visiting specialists from the Midwest to the eastern seaboard to the unrelenting emotional stress we were both burdened by, the heightened stakes in my role as a husband stole from the urgency I felt for my aspirations as a writer.

How do you wake up every morning to confront that your partner may become permanently blind that day then move on to writing about a fear of peeing in front of another man? How do you prioritize your needs to prove yourself as a man when doing so is petty and self-serving by comparison?

I was never resentful of K's vision complications, but I was worried about my identity as a writer being relegated to a frivolous hobby compared to the extra support I needed to give her to help her realize the level of success in her career that she deserved. Here was my chance to step up and be a man, to sacrifice myself for someone, and I wasn't sure I could.

Or I didn't want to.

R. W. Connell argues in *Masculinities* that men's investment in patriarchy is defended by "cultural machinery" that legitimize the authority of masculinity. "Sexism is institutionalized and state-sponsored," she argues, "enforced by social practices of violence, bullying, and peer-pressure among straight men, and enforced through physical and psychological violence against women." Kimmel says the difficulty Self-Made Men had committing to a definition of manhood measured by home and family was related to the burgeoning political awakening of the women in their lives. It's no wonder, then, that men felt threatened by the emergence of second-wave feminism that offered housewives a vision of life beyond the responsibilities to family and home assigned to them by their breadwinning husbands. There was hope for an escape for women and in this a potential end to the position of power that men held in domestic relationships.

It meant men would have to change their priorities for good.

I have to make the choice to be a good man.

I coasted to a stop in the empty back corner of the Walmart parking lot. I took a hesitant sip of my Gatorade, opened my door, and dumped the rest under my car. The tractor-trailers buzzed along the highway outside Weston. I sat and waited, just like Frank Streets had instructed me to, my eyes peeled for an unhinged sheriff who might be on the lookout for PIs and the writer-types who shadow them, particularly those who drive Blackberry Pearl–colored compact cars.

But I get ahead of myself again.

It had been about a month since Frank Streets and I had parted ways in the Staples parking lot in Clarksburg, having agreed that I would help him finish The Case of the Subject on the Run. We clearly left with different understandings of what that meant.

"He confessed everything," Frank Streets said and stared at me, his hands folded on his desk like a massive paperweight.

"So, you didn't have to do any more surveillance?" I asked in disbelief. "You didn't stake him out again? You didn't catch him doing . . . anything?"

"Nope. When the client got home from New York, the subject confessed to the affair, everything."

My mind raced. "I wonder why he admitted everything to his wife. He must have known we were following him," I asked rhetorically.

"Dunno. But they're getting a divorce." Frank Streets's voice landed like a gavel. The case was closed: confession made, divorce papers filed, Frank Streets's check written, cashed, and cleared.

A month passed and I was directionless, bogged down in the minutiae of my workaday family-man routine. I dialed Frank Streets on a whim and he picked up after two rings. "Investigation Division, this is Frank Streets," he said in his familiar gravelly voice.

"Hi, Frank, this is your old buddy Steve West," I said hopefully. At the end of our last meeting, as he escorted me through his den and out the sliding glass doors of his office, I felt panicky, like I might not see him again. He'd become the living metaphor for my aspirations as a writer. If I let him slip away, it would be me and my blank computer screen till death do us part. I needed Frank Streets.

"How's it going up in Morgantown," he replied jovially, and I exhaled.

"Good! You know, keeping busy. So, I was just calling to see what's been going on with you, see how your cases are going." I gulped. "And I wanted to see if, you know, I could follow you on another case." I clutched my breath, crossing and re-crossing my fingers several times.

"You been keeping up with the news?" I thought at first that he was making small talk to evade my request, but I could tell by his voice that his eyes were twinkling, like he was talking about ghosts.

"Not really," I simpered.

"You've missed a lot," he said with perky satisfaction. "See what's happening here in Barbour County?" Of course I hadn't. I avoided local news at all costs. I figured that if I didn't invest myself locally, it would follow that I would feel less like a local. I never read the local newspaper, never followed local elections, my gaze always up, up, and away. I dutifully remained untethered.

"What's going on?"

"It's all over the web. Just search for Barbour County Corruption." He clearly had a story he wanted to share with me, but I'd never known him to be coy. He must be involved in it somehow, I thought, when it dawned on me: he was briefing me on our next case—a story he knew I would want to write about. "Crazy stuff happening down here with the sheriff," he hinted.

"Wow, okay. I'll definitely look into it. I'll call you back, and we can maybe figure out a time I might be able to ride along with you?" I asked hopefully.

"Sure," he said, "and you can tell me what you think after you do your homework."

"Is there a test?" I joked nervously. "I'll get right on it and get back to you." I pictured Frank Streets leaned back in his chair with a wolfish smile, his fingers interlocked behind his massive head.

About a month after The Case of the Subject on the Run, eighteen-year-old Brittany Mae Keene filed a domestic violence protection order petition (DVP) against Barbour County Sheriff John Hawkins. In an article published in the Elkins newspaper, the *Inter-Mountain,* at her request, Keene went public about the relationship the two had been allegedly having over the previous year. She lambasted the sheriff, claiming that she and Hawkins dated and were "sexual partners." She also alleged that a little less than a year earlier—when she was only seventeen years old—Hawkins raped her and then threatened to have her indicted if she told anyone about it. She said the sheriff went even further, stating that he "told me my body would be the next found at Arden," a notoriously isolated enclave along the Tygart River where human remains had been discovered several times in recent years.

Within hours of the article being posted on the *Inter-Mountain* website, hundreds of comments were written debating Keene's claims. Some publicly voiced support for the sheriff, while others anonymously corroborated Keene's story with their own stories of extortion by local law enforcement. Rumors raged after Keene's accusations against the sheriff were made public; a slew of commenters shared everything from firsthand encounters with the sheriff to outlandish hearsay about local corruption on the *Inter-Mountain* website and on a discussion forum called Topix. Among these commenters, "Blue Gray Ghost" was one of the more frequent and well-informed voices responding to the accusations against the sheriff.

Within a week of the article that revealed Keene's explosive accusations against the sheriff, Blue Gray Ghost created a website of his own as a clearinghouse for information on the accusations and to foster unmediated discussion among locals. In his initial post, Blue Gray Ghost explains that many of his posts on the *Inter-Mountain* website and on Topix had been removed for being abusive and inflammatory, when they were not. If anything, his posts consistently collected the defamatory rumors circulating about the sheriff that others were making and collaged them into a coherent narrative of intrigue and conspiracy.

Blue Gray Ghost saw the removals of his posts as deliberate attempts to silence him, and he created his site to express his views unencumbered by biased censorship.

But what got me was that Blue Gray Ghost and I were on the same beat; he knew the details of the accusations against the sheriff in and out, and had insights into the case I didn't read in the news releases. He was an insider. He appeared ethical, and his opinions were rational. And his prose was well crafted. Writerly even. I bookmarked his site. I needed to keep an eye on this guy.

The comments on the *Inter-Mountain* website, Topix, and Blue Gray Ghost's blog were the homework Frank Streets had assigned me. And he was right, crazy stuff had been going on. The story was straight out of a hard-boiled detective novel: a loose cannon of a sheriff accused of exploiting his authority for sex, and a corrupt local justice system dragged into the spotlight by a teenage girl with nothing to lose in taking the threats made against her public.

And Keene may not have been the only one: just the first one willing to voice the abuse she endured. After a thorough, objective overview of the story—including a clinical breakdown of the timeline from the Barbour County prosecutor's initial denial that Keene's DVP was filed to protect her from the sheriff to his denial of that denial after Keene took her accusations public—Blue Gray Ghost shifted his tone from one of rational deduction to conspiratorial provocation. "It does indeed look like there was an effort to hide certain aspects if not all of them. Which makes me wonder," Blue Gray Ghost mused, "what else is there that could be hidden?"

Nothing I read mentioned how Franklin D. Streets, private investigator, was connected, other than that it was all unfolding in his backyard. I concluded that he had to be working the case. But how? I knew he wouldn't be working for the county, and certainly not in the sheriff's defense. The Barbour County Sheriff's Department was the same outfit he had worked for briefly as a sheriff's deputy prior to becoming a PI, the place where he said he saw too much corruption that got in the way of "true justice." That couldn't be his angle.

I reread the story on the *Inter-Mountain* from the beginning and noticed that Keene's attorney was Paul Harris. The name rang a bell. Harris was the lawyer out of Wheeling that Frank Streets regularly worked for on criminal cases, his "buddy" he talked to on the phone several times when we worked the case of the adulterer, calling him about their "corrupt little town" of Shinnston in reference to their work together on the Junkins case and the cops trading drugs for sex; it was his conversation with Paul Harris in downtown Clarksburg that was the reason we had lost the subject that day.

Paul Harris was defending Keene, so Frank Streets had to be working the case. That was it: Frank Streets was investigating the accusations Keene had made against the Barbour County Sheriff. I got nervous thinking about it. I'd driven through swaths of Barbour County several times on my way to find Valley View Road and Frank Streets, and it was remote to say the least. It was too easy to imagine that if I tagged along with Frank Streets on his investigation of the sheriff my body might be the next one found in Arden, if it was found at all.

K's loss of vision shook me. I was overtaken with the fear that the laser treatment might not hold, that she could be totally blind at any time. Every day, this fear, this vulnerability, this helplessness. What could I do to stop it? And what could I do to help her?

But over time it became the new normal as we reoriented our lives around the change in her vision. I stopped asking twice a day if the flashes were back. I always drove. I sat exclusively on her left side. I stopped tossing keys to her. I encouraged her to buy new glasses with expensive lenses. I examined snow falling, the current on the river, the smoke unfurling from chimneys with both eyes open, and then always with one closed, to share it with her, even when she wasn't with me. Especially then.

At first we tried to live like we used to—meaning we were denying what had changed. We went to see *Synecdoche, New York* a few months after her vision loss, when her right eye was still pointing toward her nose while her left looked straight ahead. I dragged her to watch that movie because I love Charlie Kauffman. (*Adaptation* is one of my all-time favorites; it's the second-best film about a man failing to make the art he envisions—to be the man the world expects him to be—after Ross McElwee's *Sherman's March*, obviously.)

K had a difficult time tracking the images on the big screen, and the effort made her experience vertigo, but she is not one for confessions; she kept that devastating confrontation with how her life had changed to herself.

Almost a year later, when her right eye no longer pointed inward and she moved on from life in three dimensions, we decided to try going to a movie again, having learned to sit as far back and to the right as possible. It was early January, just a few weeks from my thirty-first birthday, a newspaper sky.

"I'm late."

I looked at the clock on the dash. "What do you mean? We still have about thirty minutes." My throat constricted. I jerked the wheel.

"How late."

"Two weeks."

I steered into a CVS parking lot. K and I went in together and bought a box of the cheapest pregnancy tests we could find.

The theater connected to the mall food court, so K dashed into the bathroom before we bought tickets. I stood in the middle of the food court, staring down the tile corridor, forcing my diaphragm up and down in an approximation of breathing, blinking through the flashing lights of the merry-go-round, the mingling smells of soft pretzel and orange chicken stir-fry.

She peed on a test stick. There was a line.

She peed on another stick, and there was another line.

We were going to have a baby.

I was going to be a father.

I don't usually get emotional while watching movies. The last movie that made me cry was *Mr. Holland's Opus*. I was fifteen years old, and it hit me hard. I might have been on medication, I don't remember. But now, of course I see it as a premonition. What do we know about what will define us in the end? Could the seed of my fear of failing as an artist and as a man have been planted then, by a weathered Richard Dreyfuss as he treated his family like shit in the face of his failed ambition?

Life was deliberate and floaty and in slow motion like footage of a lunar landing for both K and me, but we bought our tickets for *Black Swan* anyway. We sat in silence next to each other for two hours with our soda and popcorn and two positive pregnancy tests and everything in the world to talk about. And I cried. And not to take anything away from Natalie Portman's moving performance as an artist so driven by her ambition that when given the chance she'd dreamed of she has to cleave her identity to fulfill her desire to the point that it destroys her, but I cried because I was going to be a father.

I was going to be a father, and I scrambled for something to write about, to cast a solid shape to define me before that definition was irrevocably changed. I started thinking about Sophie Calle and dreaming about Bob Clay following me around. It was almost a year from that day that I met Frank Streets.

I sat facing the entrance of the Walmart parking lot. A large camper towing a Geo Tracker pulled in and drove slowly toward me, coming to a stop perpendicular to the front of my car. I watched as a side door opened and a single flip-flop tumbled out, a teenage girl following close behind. With one flip-flop still on, she leaned over slowly to pick up the other, and carried it as she slouched her way to the Tracker. My eyes followed her parents from the cab of the camper to the Tracker, where they fished out some items and then walked with their daughter toward Walmart.

I looked at the clock then back to the entrance to the lot. I watched as a black Ford Escape with tinted windows pulled in and slowly circled around the camper. It came to a stop off to the right of the camper, and I could see the silhouettes of two men in the cab of the vehicle. The massive frame in the driver seat could only have belonged to one man.

I started my car and eased toward them; the lot was still empty enough that Frank Streets and the other man noticed me and stared together as I pulled up next to them and rolled down my window.

"I didn't recognize you at first in that vehicle," I said with a wide smile.

"Just got it the other day," Frank Streets said harshly without cracking a smile. My teeth suddenly felt big, and I closed my lips over them.

Coupled with his mirrored aviator sunglasses and crisp white button-down, Frank Streets's high and tight flattop and short goatee gave him an edge of toughness that I didn't remember when we chased the adulterer together. The look of his operation had jumped forward in television history by at least a decade. My stomach dropped; it had been only a few months since I'd last seen him, but I felt like I had to start over with this Frank Streets.

I grabbed my bag and walked toward the back of the Escape and climbed in the rear passenger side. "Thanks for meeting me here," I said nervously.

"This is one of my guys," Frank Streets replied without looking at the man in the front passenger seat. "His name's Jim. He's gonna be working with us today."

I was disappointed it wasn't Half-Unit. I leaned awkwardly toward the middle of the backseat as Jim twisted in the front seat and stuck his hand back to me. I shook it.

"Nice to meet you," he said with a thick Appalachian accent, his wide face as unmoved as his voice. Jim had a brush cut, a clean shave, and his sharp blue eyes contrasted with the tanned and acne-scarred skin of his cheeks and neck. Like Frank Streets, he also wore a pressed short-sleeve button-down, but it looked more like something from a JCPenney outlet, light beige and patternless. He was more intimidating than Half-Unit, as in he actually looked like a PI. Frank Streets and Jim both looked more like lawyers than people ready to pee in a bottle at a moment's notice. I felt shabby in my teaching uniform of a wrinkled plaid oxford and faded khakis.

"Nice car," I said automatically as I leaned back into my seat and buckled in. The interior was a palette of grays and blacks, and it still had that stiff newness to it. Frank Streets drove out of the parking lot. We stopped at the light at the end of the street, where it intersected with U.S. 50. We sat in silence.

If I felt nervous about the changes in Frank Streets physical appearance and outward demeanor, and the fact that I was in the backseat and closed out of the conversation didn't help. I felt like an important part of the investigation in the case of the adulterer—like a sidekick—but today I felt left out, like I didn't belong. Our rapport was gone, and I wondered if it had ever actually existed. I was a writer, Frank Streets was a PI, and this was business.

I didn't know what case Frank Streets was working today; all I knew was that we weren't working the case of the sheriff; to my simultaneous disappointment and relief, Frank Streets decided at the last minute that he wouldn't let me tag along on that one. That situation had become so volatile that federal agents were called in to aid in the investigation, and Frank Streets was working in tandem with an FBI agent he referred to as "Fast Freddie."

Fast Freddie had attached himself to Frank Streets's operation because he couldn't get anywhere near the level of access to information about the sheriff that Frank Streets could. The locals knew and trusted Frank Streets, and he could find people in the obscure hollows of Barbour County and get them to talk far more easily than a fed from D.C. could ever dream of. Frank Streets is smart and professional, but he is West Virginian through and through, and if potential witnesses were scared stiff of getting on the bad side of a sheriff who was rumored to do anything to keep people quiet, they certainly wouldn't expose themselves to an outsider. Frank Streets was the key to any story Fast Freddie might uncover, and that's why he needed him. Why I needed him.

Impulsively, I leaned forward and stuck my head between the front seats. "So, this case we're working on took place right around here?" I wanted to seem confident; maybe it would conjure some of the familiarity I believed I'd earned with Frank Streets.

"Yup," he replied curtly.

"Took place here," I continued awkwardly. "With people around here?"

"Jane Lew," Frank Streets reluctantly offered. "Took place in Jane Lew." In the past, these small prompts would have been enough to get Frank Streets spilling his guts about the case, including all the background information he had as well as what he still needed to get. Stiff silence returned to the cab of the Escape.

"The defendant's name is Christopher Sheppard," he said, breaking the silence. He enunciated the name deliberately as if he knew I was writing it down. It rang a bell—it was from a case of a murdered toddler that Frank Streets had described when I'd last ridden along with him. "It's all over the papers and everything," he muttered. That was for Jim; he wanted him to know why he was sharing this information with the writer in the backseat. I realized that was why Frank Streets wasn't chatting my ear off; it wasn't about our relationship; it was about the dynamic of having one of his employees in the vehicle, akin to his surly responses to Joanne and Half-Unit. I urged the feeling back into my stomach.

"Christopher Sheppard, the boy accused of the murder, he told me the other day that he literally saw the mother pick up and slam the child. He said he was bathing the child, and the child fell out of the sink, that's his story. But prior to that the mother had thrown it." Frank Streets tilted his head to look at me with a sidelong glance. "In the autopsy, they found all the baby's ribs were broken before," he said, evaluating my reaction. "I got all the autopsy pictures. I mean we're dealing with the murder of a little baby." I could see by the way he frowned and shook his head that he was not excited to look at those autopsy pictures. And who could blame him.

"Sheppard said the mother's nothing but a crack whore," he continued. "I don't want to work the case to get Sheppard off from killing the baby. I know the boy's guilty. He said if the prosecutor walked in and offered him fifteen to twenty years, he'd take it. So, he has to be guilty of some of it. But then again, I want to work it to make sure I get everyone who was involved." Frank Streets paused, measuring his words to mute what I'd already heard: he had an angle he was after.

As we turned on to 119 heading away from Walmart, Jim

leaned into the middle of the Escape. He sneered at Frank Streets. "So, you wouldn't allow him to watch you work the sheriff case, huh?"

"Oh my god—that's just what I need is for him to get shot," Frank Streets said dramatically.

I laughed and chimed in, "Yeah, I'm alright with not being shot."

"You'd have to give him a bulletproof vest." Jim chuckled and bobbed in his seat.

"I'm dead serious," Frank Streets added excitedly. "We've been riding around all week with a loaded shotgun and everything."

"That's a hairy situation down there," I said, trying to sound like an insider.

"It is," Frank Streets nodded slowly. "He said he's gonna take somebody out and take himself out." The sheriff.

"That threat could be total bullshit," Jim said dismissively. This was evidence that everyone in Frank Streets's outfit was silently thinking about the sheriff no matter what case they were working on. A suicidal–homicidal sheriff would be at the forefront of my mind, too.

Jim cocked his head, as if weighing evidence. "Or, it could be real." We sat in silence, my mind a montage of movies featuring corrupt cops who go on killing rampages before turning the gun on themselves.

"When someone's threatening to shoot at you, I think you take the threat as real," Jim added quizzically as Frank Streets stamped the gas, the Escape roaring as it accelerated. "Then you hope it's bullshit."

"I'm happy investigating a murdered baby," I chirped, sitting back and pulling my seatbelt tight for emphasis, my weenie writer routine coming quite naturally as the dark irony of what I had just said landed with a thud. "So, this case we're investigating today, how was the baby murdered?"

"Basically beat to death," Jim stated. "Depends on what version of the story you're told."

When a fifteen-month-old baby named Rex was killed in Jane Lew, a hamlet tucked among the mountains northeast of Weston, Frank Streets was hired by the attorney defending Christopher Sheppard, the twenty-two-year-old charged with killing the baby. According to pre-hearing testimony, Sheppard was watching Rex while his girlfriend, Julie Mick—the mother of the child—was out of the house. Sheppard claimed he left the baby unattended while he was bathing him in the kitchen sink, when the baby fell out and landed on his head. When Julie returned home to find her son Rex unresponsive, she called 911—but only after a cold rag and a frozen can of juice wouldn't wake him.

Rex died at the hospital after emergency brain surgery, with the cause of death being blunt force trauma. During the autopsy, the coroner noted that the baby had numerous bruises and injuries to the mouth and face and freshly broken ribs. Sheppard said in statements to the police that the baby was choking when he found him, so he administered CPR, which supposedly resulted in the broken ribs. That explanation didn't account for the five ribs that were in various stages of healing from a previous injury, according to the autopsy report.

"You trying to catch up with some witnesses today?" I leaned forward and asked hopefully.

Frank Streets shook his head with a flourish. "Trying to find three women. Mariela Call, and two that go by Pick and Fee." Frank Streets pursed his broad lips. "They're lesbians and they live together or something." The fat way it landed, I could tell the L-word felt unfamiliar coming out of his mouth. Jim sat silently. "Apparently they hung around with the mother a lot around the time the baby was murdered." Frank Streets frowned. "She sounds like a piece of trash, going from boyfriend to boyfriend." I wasn't sure why Frank Streets was interested in bad-mouthing the mom; it was pretty clear that Sheppard had killed the baby, at least from everything I'd learned about the story and what Frank Streets had told me.

"So, my thing is the autopsy shows five other ribs that had been mending for some time," Frank Streets said, cutting to the chase. "Was it during the time before our guy got there? If so, then there's someone else guilty of prior abuse against that child." It took me a second to register that "our guy" was Sheppard, and I instinctively recoiled back into my seat. We were working for the murderer.

"Now, I'm not trying to get our guy completely off," Frank Streets stated diplomatically. "Absolutely not. He was there. But the courts aren't even thinking about charging the mother. The police aren't investigating her at all. The prosecutor has got so many cases right now," he continued. "He says he's got five murder cases, that he doesn't have time to worry about this case since he's got a pretty strong conviction on Sheppard. But the thing about it is the mother wasn't even there when this was supposed to have happened," he said. "She was out buying drugs or doing something." The disgust in his voice was palpable. I could see that we weren't interested in learning more about Sheppard's involvement in the murder at all today; that was a forgone conclusion. We were out for dirt on the murdered baby's mother.

Frank Streets had told me before that he doesn't care what the people who hire him want him to look for; he said his responsibility is to uncover everything he can about the people involved in a case he is investigating. It's how he remains ethical as an investigator, he said.

I can relate because I am also drawn to uncover everything I can—even items that feel unnecessary—those, especially, sometimes—in an exhaustive way. It is not popular, and I get it (see: my MFA thesis), but I can't stop digging into art that prioritizes process over product, like Kenneth Goldsmith's book *Day*, where he retyped every single word of an edition of the *New York Times*, from the top left to the bottom right of every single goddamn page, not discriminating among articles and advertisements nor paying heed to typographical variation. The result? 836 pages of "uncreative writing," as he called it. But Goldsmith was being coy, of course; in his effort to eliminate his decision-making as a writer, he was making a stylistic choice and he knew it: Goldsmith was shaping an argument even in his commitment to unshaping. That he said in an interview that he expected to "cleanse himself of all creativity" through the project just highlights this.

Like Frank Streets, I chase every lead in a project, uncovering everything I can. And like Kenneth Goldsmith, I operate automatically when it comes to documenting and cataloguing what I discover. iPhone notes and scraps of thought; screen captures and browser bookmarks; albums of unartful photographs of empty roads and blurry dashboards, of PIs peeing freely with no bottle in sight; pages of transcribed audio recordings of interviews I will never share; and all the dead leads I've loved along the way. But I will not be coy. I know that my art is not your art, dear reader, and Kenneth Goldsmith might be my only audience for the slew of unordered documents that make up the unshaped mass of work on my hard drive.

Frank Streets told me that a client can piece together the information he finds in whatever way they want. He said if he eliminated his personal desire from influencing his work it also alleviated him from being responsible for the impact his investigations had on the lives of the people involved.

But no one makes art for themselves alone, not even you, Ken, and no PI investigates someone for his own amusement. A writer needs a reader, and an investigator needs a client, and both need to deliver a story. Frank Streets's summary of his process is noble, but, like Goldsmith, he was being coy and he knew it. He knew he was the character in the story I was writing, and he wanted to shape that character for me. But on the trail of Rex's murder, I had a feeling that Frank Streets was out for information that confirmed a story he already believed — or at least wanted to find. Frank Streets and I are the same in that way.

❖

K and I hadn't planned on getting pregnant when we did, but we had always talked about maybe having kids, eventually, after our careers were in full swing. Maybe. She was more convinced she wanted to be a parent than I was. I knew that I was self-involved, and I worried about how much I would have to take away from myself to give to a child. I was reluctant about that commitment. It wasn't a need I had, and to be honest, I'm not sure I ever would have decided I was ready to be a father.

Throughout K's pregnancy, I toiled with anxiety like I hadn't since I was a teen afraid of what I might do to the people I loved in the middle of the night. What if I got so anxious about the changes in my priorities that I ran away from K, from our baby, from all the best things I had going for me? What if I got so frustrated when the baby wouldn't stop crying that my field of vision went red? My imagination always darted to the darkest outcomes, and I was overwhelmed with guilt for atrocities I hadn't committed.

Over the nine months that followed our fraught viewing of *Black Swan*, I managed my anxiety with practical tasks I could control. If it's a cliché that an expectant mother will invest herself in nesting for a new baby's arrival—picking out clothes and buying a recliner for breastfeeding and so on—I upped the ante by renovating the entire second floor of our house, from sanding and refinishing the previously carpeted and painted wood floors to painting every single surface with thick, bright colors.

Michael Kimmel observes that by the mid-twentieth century, Self-Made Men's role in the family sphere expanded to include domestic responsibilities traditionally assigned to women: cleaning, cooking, and, of course, child-rearing. These new roles beyond bringer-home-of-the-bacon didn't come without costs to manhood. "Responsible breadwinners and devoted fathers," he opines of mid-twentieth-century men in the mold of Ward

Cleaver, "were anxious about overconformity but unable and unwilling to break free of domestic responsibilities."

If I feared what the commitment I made to K after her vision loss meant for my aspirations as a writer, El represented that ten times over. To be settled and stable, to live the risk-reduced lifestyle that would support K and her career and provide El with the upbringing I thought he deserved felt like a direct threat to the dreams I'd coddled since I was a tween painting moody self-portraits and scribbling melodramatic poetry. What energy could I dedicate to being a writer, what time to the projects that I had spent my life caring about more than anything in the world when El needed all of my attention?

But even if the fundamental shift in my priorities to supporting El and K was the blunt announcement that art would only ever be ancillary to my *Leave It to Beaver* identity, I knew that wouldn't translate into me being a deadbeat dad. I just didn't have it in me. I had to grow into the role, and it took work. It still feels like work. But it's work I am proud of. My life doesn't have new meaning. It's the same old life, and I'm the same old me; I am still self-interested; I still feel lost; I don't believe I was put on this earth for any single purpose— talk about pressure—but I do think I'm doing the best I can by being honest with myself that I don't always love being a parent.

Since El was born, every moment of my life had a pall of practical necessity looming over it in a way it didn't before. I have the responsibility to provide love and support for an absurdly dependent little person whose existence I am responsible for. He had no choice in the matter. After K's eye surgery I had to put her needs before mine, but she was an adult and strong and independent and I could trust she'd be fine without me. But with El, his life was literally in my hands. That is some serious shit.

But caring for him came easy, and I felt relieved when I realized that. Even if I am obsessed with myself, I am a caretaker, and I thrive when people need my help.

But I still have my *Black Swan* moments of self-centered desire that bristle at the responsibility I have as a spouse and parent, and that's why Rex's fate haunted me.

El was now the same age as Rex would have been when his ribs were broken. Sometimes when I feel El's soft ribcage give when I hook my hands under his armpits and lift, I feel how vulnerable he is and how much he trusts me, and I think of Rex, of what cloud could possibly come over me to make me lose control and hurt him, because I cannot empathize with someone who could do it intentionally.

When I visited the Empire State Building as a preteen, it was an overcast day with low visibility, the wisps of clouds blowing through me and over the ledge of the observation deck. I was reluctant to get close to the edge of the viewing platform, suddenly struck by the fear that I might jump. There were easily more than enough chain link fences, nets, and security guards to thwart even the most dedicated jumper, let alone a kid impulsively flinging himself off, but my stomach constricted like a mussel and my limbs tingled at the thought that I just might find a way. What if I impulsively jumped, an outcome inspired by mysterious internal forces, those that in theory I could control? Even if there was only a one in a billion chance I would throw myself off, I couldn't convince myself to believe it could never happen.

Around that time, I would lie quiet and still in bed at night, my breathing shallow, trying to convince the knot in my stomach to untie itself. Sometimes I would sob and dry heave, rubbing my forehead until my skin got hot to the touch. How could I know I wouldn't wake up in the dead of night and kill myself? How could I know I wouldn't grab a knife from the kitchen, butcher my parents and siblings as they slept before gashing my own throat? I couldn't imagine doing it, but I couldn't absolutely know that I wouldn't. On more histrionic nights, my mom would climb in bed with me and rub my back, our foreheads touching as she sang "Fire and Rain," "Blowin' in the Wind," "Bridge over Troubled Water," the lyrics trembling in her throat with what I like to think was her frustration that she could never really know what had me so worked up. Or her fear that she did.

When I rock El to sleep, his head tucked warm and tight in the crook of my arm, sometimes I sing those songs to him, and I hope that someday he doesn't feel like I did, like I do, that he won't be able to empathize with me, but he will understand that I am only doing what I think is right by openly sharing my fears like this, trying the only way I know how to become the kind of father he deserves.

The inability that men feel to meet the expectation that they must toggle between their roles as both fathers and breadwinners — and really, the idea that these identities are in competition in the first place — is a strain on the male psyche. "Especially," Kimmel chides — and I agree with him here — "when many fathers weren't very good at child rearing and had been so poorly trained for it." The separation of responsibilities by gender within households had become so entrenched in the mid-twentieth century that men who had spent the majority of their lives building identities around work and public standing had spent little time or energy developing the skills necessary for successful nurturing of children. Patience. Compassion. Tenderness. Attention to process. The cultural education men had received from the cradle assured that they were mostly hopeless failures when it came to these traits.

And to this day, most married, straight men have difficulty forging a sense of "manly" accomplishment in their roles as fathers. Sure, there is Coach Dad, but how else? When the emotional lives of their wives and children arrive, the ability to listen, empathize, and provide support is not as easy as playing catch in the yard. Kimmel says that men experienced "restless anxiety" as a result of the demand to prioritize family alongside career advancement; "all that sober responsibility,"

Kimmel concludes, "left a gaping void in the hearts of men, where once adventure, risk, and sexual passion had reigned." The belief that the Self-Made Man could find a secure sense of masculinity in being a successful breadwinner, sober family man, and swashbuckling hero was finally exposed as a fraud.

"As men felt their real sense of masculinity eroding," Kimmel writes, "they turned to fantasies that embodied heroic physical action." Spectator sports like baseball and football rocketed in popularity, and men sampled bygone tropes of masculinity in tales of "men being men" found in dime-store novels. These escapist reads imagined worlds where brave cowboys tamed the wild frontier and hard-nosed detectives cracked cases, where success was available to the most enterprising, the most powerful, the most brutal and self-made among them.

"Self-Made Men longed to make themselves all over again," Kimmel writes. "In both fiction and fact, they ran away."

As we slowed and entered Jane Lew, its downtown materialized in familiar fashion: a faded gas station, a diner with greasy windows, a video gambling bar, a series of two-story storefronts with a staccato of old brick and soiled plastic siding, their ad hoc sequence of flat and peaked roofs revealing architectural decisions made by necessity, not aesthetic.

Jane Lew is the epitome of the minute towns scattered across the landscape of central West Virginia. According to the latest census, it is home to 380 people. It is not a ghost town, even if that description feels apt.

"There it is," Frank Streets announced. I quickly spied our destination on our left, T & L HOT DOGS written in ketchup-red on a bun-colored plastic sign, the chipping paint most noticeable in the image of a smiling hot dog skewering itself.

Frank Streets maneuvered us into the cramped lot alongside T & L, the power steering moaning as he inched the front bumper up to the red bricks of the building to keep our tailgate out of the alleyway. He yanked the parking brake and pulled out his notebook from the center console. Jim and I sat in silence as he flipped through his notes.

Frank Streets slammed his notebook back into the console. "We're gonna go in," he said as he opened the door and jumped out with an agility surprising for a man his size.

"Do you want me to stay in the car?" I asked nervously.

"No. You're just one of my associates," Frank Streets said coolly. In the car, I was a weenie writer, but in public, I was a PI.

"I'll look real grim, you know," I said and chuckled self-consciously. I furrowed my brow and drew the line of my mouth taught, forging myself into my new role. It was 9:37 am.

Jim and I followed Frank Streets as he burst through the front doors. The small dining room was tiled in white and outlined with red linoleum booths. It was empty. I certainly wouldn't be in the mood to eat a hot dog at this time of the morning, but two young women were standing alertly behind the counter ready to take our order. They wore unmatched T-shirts, gym shorts, and aprons, and looked to be in their teens.

"How you ladies doing?" Frank Streets asked, leaning heavily on the chest-high counter.

"Good, how are you," the taller of the two replied in the sing-songy way teenagers who work in food service do, without a hint of sincerity. I noticed the greasy image of the smiling hot dog from the sign on the breast of her shirt. She was thin and blond, pretty in a way, but not remarkably so. Her upper lip was pierced with a diamond stud.

"Trying to find some information," Frank Streets announced gruffly, filling the tiny dining room with his presence. Jim and I hung back, and I tried to match the sternly disinterested look on his face. Jim took a few deliberately moseying steps to our left and tilted his head to get a better angle on the dining area. He stood a few feet away from me, and I stayed where I was and looked around suspiciously. I crossed my arms and tried to widen my stance, imagining I was shaped like a V behind Frank Streets as he began to interrogate the girls.

"You ever heard of a girl named Pick?" Frank Streets folded his hands on the countertop, stretching his fingers out before slowly weaving them together like he was shuffling a deck of cards. He tilted his head and squinted. Both girls stood very still. I fidgeted on the balls of my feet. The shorter girl was stockier than Diamond Stud, her thick black hair exploding from her ponytail in a frantic spiral of ringlets. Her thick eyebrows pointed sharply toward a crease that split her eyes while she listened. She had a tattoo of a peace sign on her shoulder.

"Yes, I have," Diamond Stud replied slowly. Peace Sign had no idea who Pick was and walked back to the kitchen, visible through the serving window. She stirred a stainless-steel cauldron that steamed aggressively, and I pictured dozens of hot dogs swirling in a bubbling vortex of brownish water.

"How about a girl named Fee?" Frank Streets asked. Diamond Stud stared.

Jim wandered behind us to a second small dining room that opened to the left of the counter. He was casing the joint. I crossed my arms like a tough guy, purposefully squinting and flexing my jaw. A door creaked loudly behind me; I snapped around in time to see Jim strut into the restroom.

"Fee?" Frank Streets repeated to crack her demeanor. "I think it's short for Stephanie?" Diamond Stud finally broke form and shook her head. "Pick and Fee," Frank Streets continued, "I guess they're lesbians," he mumbled. "Now Rodney Weaver, Jr., he used to hang out with this Julia Mick?"

"Yeah, he used to live with her," Diamond Stud said confidently. "Rodney, his step-mom owns this place, and Rodney— Skinny, they call him—he comes in here sometimes. But they don't hear from him a whole lot. The last I heard he was in a halfway house somewhere trying to get clean. He hasn't really been wanted around a whole lot because he steals her jewelry and everything else."

Frank Streets laughed robustly and looked at the ceiling.

"What do you know about Pick?"

"I think she lives in Lost Creek. She comes in here every now and then to get hot dogs, but that's only once every few months or so. I know about where her mom and dad live because I was dating one of her relatives. I don't know anything else about her. I know she came in here, but I haven't seen her in a long time."

"What about a Mariela? Mariela Call." Frank Streets eyed Diamond Stud.

"I know Pick, but I don't know anybody else she's . . . related to," Diamond Stud said, avoiding the L-word. Jim squeaked his way out of the bathroom, and Peace Sign stirred the boiling hot dogs. Diamond Stud shook her head and laughed uncomfortably. She cocked her head.

"You probably already know what all of this is about, don't you?" Frank Streets stared hard at her. "The baby?"

"Who?"

"Rex? Over here at the Jane Lew Apartments? Only thirteen months old?" She shook her head slowly, thinking. "Christopher Sheppard? The one we arrested and put in jail?" Frank Streets's use of "we" hit a discordant note: "we" had incarcerated Christopher Sheppard, making "us" law enforcement. I didn't think much of it, though—it was all the same to Diamond Stud and Peace Sign. We walked in, and they just started talking. It's not like we were coercing them to answer our questions.

"That little Rex, he died." Frank Street continued. "Up there at Jane Lew Apartments."

"I remember that, now that you're saying it."

"What's got me concerned about that case," Frank Streets continued, "is when they did the autopsy the baby had six broken ribs that were mending, way prior to Sheppard coming in." Diamond Stud shook her head, a defeated and knowing look on her face. "Well, you've been quite the help," Frank Streets said abruptly and spun on his heel to leave.

I saw an opportunity. "I'll be right out," I yelped and skipped over to the restroom. I pushed out a pee as quickly as I could, flushed, and washed my hands in one continuous motion, then strutted back through the dining area toward the door. I shrugged awkwardly in the direction of the girls. I didn't say thank you. I didn't say goodbye. I didn't want my voice to crack or sound froggy, revealing that none of us were police detectives, or that I was just a paper tiger of a writer with no real business digging into the overlapping tragedies of these people's lives.

"Here's a little tip, when you're riding with Frank, and you have five seconds to take a leak, you take it. He leaks about once every three weeks, whether he needs to go or not. And then, wherever you're at, the stream rises about six inches."

"That's the truth," Frank Streets said proudly and buckled his seatbelt.

"That's the running joke with us," Jim said and smiled at Frank Streets as we pulled out of the T & L HOT DOGS parking lot. "If we're near a restroom I'm gonna go whether I need to or not, and if I have to stand there and wait five minutes for a couple dribbles, I'm gonna do it." Jim and I were clearly kindred spirits in our anxiety about peeing in Frank Streets's vicinity.

He looked at Frank Streets. "She was just full of information for you."

"Yes, she was," Frank Streets replied quietly. "She liked me," he quipped.

"She wanted your body."

"Oh yeah, I could tell. I'm feeling this flattop, perfect fit."

"Not a six-pack, but a twelve-pack." Jim joked.

"I didn't lie to her once!" Frank Streets exclaimed out of nowhere, like he was defending himself. "I'm out of Barbour County and I've been assigned this case." He chuckled nervously.

"Mr. Law Enforcement," Jim chirped.

"I did not say law enforcement," Frank Streets bellowed in protest.

Jim sneered and bared his teeth. "I didn't say you did."

"I never said a word. What she thinks is her prerogative."

"I think I got included in law enforcement there," I chimed in. "First and last time."

"You're a cop," Frank Streets accused me dramatically.

"Do I look like a cop, honey?" Jim mocked.

"Gonna have to get him a gun," Frank Street said soberly.

"Look at the guy with the flattop. You look like a cop when you're standing next to him," Frank Streets said and laughed, and I felt about half his size.

"Maybe you can start carrying the shotgun around," Jim suggested.

Frank Streets gestured to the backseat with his head as we started driving back toward the highway. "It's right behind you." I didn't turn around.

I took note that Frank Streets was so wary of what he had said and how it might have been interpreted; no one had accused him of misrepresenting himself, but he was acting like it anyway, like he was thinking what I was thinking, that the lies we rely on aren't always harmless fabrications.

The accusation Frank Streets was defending himself against came from within, and I could relate. The lies we create about ourselves are casts from the mold of our ideal selves, the hero-forms each of us desires to be, and sometimes we even begin to believe in them.

Like being a PI inspired to find justice, not just the story he wants to be true.

Like being a writer inspired to reveal the truth, not just a good story.

Like being a man not just motivated to serve his fragile ego, but to care for those who actually need it.

And if Frank Streets was thinking what I was thinking, then he was wary of how closely I was listening and watching him, because I worry that the truth can be harmed by intentionality.

Jim grabbed a handful of Mentos and stuffed them in his mouth. He chewed for a minute, then turned and looked at me. "Can you tell me what you're doing this research for?" He moved the wad of mints to his cheek. "I know you're gonna write a story, right?"

"I'm writing a book," I began convincingly. "I'm interested in how the work private investigators do parallels what writers do. They gotta research, gotta find a ton of information, gotta go out in the field, like right now for example, I'm following you guys around, taking notes, making assumptions, trying to draw conclusions." Jim chewed and nodded, the crease that divided his forehead lengthwise deepening between his eyes. Frank Streets adjusted in his seat.

"It's kind of a more creative piece of writing," I added, hoping it would sound as flaccid to them as it did to me and defuse any concern my "observing and trying to draw conclusions" might create.

"Gotcha."

"It won't be done for a while." Jim turned around and faced forward, satisfied. I sensed that Frank Streets was listening, so I felt compelled to continue. "I also think it's interesting to observe what you guys do because we're in West Virginia, which you know, all the detective stories people read, all the corruption usually takes place in a city like New York or L.A."

"It's just as prevalent in a small town." Jim said quickly. "Just as prevalent, if not more so."

"And when you find it here in West Virginia," Frank Streets interrupted, "it's interwoven into everything. The mayor is somebody's brother-in-law, the chief of police is somebody's uncle. It's just everywhere. Everything's corrupt here."

"And when it's taking place somewhere isolated, you can feel helpless," I added, the suddenly amplified nuances of the road a nod to the relativity of silence. I thought of K and El and moved my hand compulsively into a patch of light on the seat next to me, to feel its warmth.

"A statement was made last week when we were working the sheriff case," Frank Streets snarled, "that when all of the police are involved in something, when you are truly in trouble, who do you go to? Who do you go to and say help me?"

This sheriff was invoking real fear in the people. Even Jim and Frank Streets, two hard-nosed PIs carrying sidearms, wearing bulletproof vests, and driving around with a shotgun in the backseat were willing to admit that they hoped his threats were empty. They were scared, and I sensed the pall of fear that had hung over the region since the sheriff's threats against Keene came out.

"Are there more girls out there that are going to claim that Hawkins had sex with them?" Blue Gray Ghost asks in one of his blog posts where he meditates on the way the retribution people fear if they speak out keeps them silent, and how that thwarts the true depths of corruption ever being exposed.

Blue Gray Ghost suggests yet again that there are more young women than just Keene with stories to tell about the sheriff. "The evidence that supports my statement lies within the numerous emails that I have received," he suggests. "Each of which has in fact referred to fear as being the main motive for not coming forward. It is with threats of violence that not only creates a web of fear but a circle of silence," Blue Gray Ghost laments, "essentially keeping others from stepping forward."

I'm an educated white man of average physical stature, and I would be afraid to speak out against the sheriff. And these "others" Blue Gray Ghost calls out are undoubtedly from disadvantaged and disempowered backgrounds. "Maybe there are more that we do not know about," Blue Gray Ghost suggests, "maybe people with credibility issues that if challenged would be put at a disadvantage as compared to the respectful position of sheriff? Hawkins supporters have described Keene as a girl with no credibility," he continues. "That is of course the exact kind of person that a predator would seek out; someone who has a disadvantageous background that would make their statements suspect and allow a person of higher caliber to be believed."

I could only imagine the terror any of these young women experienced each day, let alone at the thought of what might happen if no one believed their stories and the sheriff pulled into their driveways to tell them so. There is excessively more at stake for real victims than for a writer who chooses to nudge them into the light, even through subtle allusions to their existence and their claims.

"I do not wish to give the impression that speaking out is free from hardship because frankly it is not a path so easily maintained," Blue Gray Ghost writes in anticipation of this criticism, "for there are many obstacles to contend with such as ridicule, harassment, and intimidation. Is any road to honesty, truth or freedom an easy task? I think we all know the answer to that is no!" But really, Blue Gray Ghost—how hard is it to pursue the truth when you have the privilege of being a man and a writer—especially a writer who provokes his audience with meditations on the real, tragic corruption, the real, tragic lives of disadvantaged groups of people in trouble from behind the safety of a computer screen?

Escapist reading wasn't merely appealing to the status quo among a generation of men. In an essay he wrote for *Harper's* in the late 1940s, W. H. Auden confesses that "the reading of detective stories is an addiction like tobacco or alcohol." Auden is referring to "whodunits," the genteel turn-of-the-century mystery stories that featured resourceful and rational genius–detectives that typically encounter a surprise corpse or two in a cottage in the English countryside. These stories invite the reader to ride shotgun with a charming sleuth like Sherlock Holmes or Father Brown or Hercule Poirot while he unravels the clues the murderer left behind to reveal the guilty party and motive in an aha! payoff at the very end.

In these detective stories," Auden writes, "the audience does not know the truth at all; the detective, of his own free will, discovers and reveals what the murderer, of his own free will, tries to conceal." In a detective story, the decisive event—the crime—has already occurred, and it is only a matter of time before the truth is revealed. "Time and space," Auden claims, "are simply the when and where of revealing either what has to happen or what has actually happened." There is no escape, in other words; the outcome is fated by the actions that preceded the narrative.

Auden suggests that, like Greek tragedy, detective stories differ from modern tragedy in that the characters are never transformed through the events that unfold in the story. This is not the intent of the detective story at all; in fact, for Auden, a detective or a villain that is changed by way of their actions would betray the purpose of the story, the very escapism they are written to foster.

Despite this one commonality with tragedy, Auden thinks detective stories have about as much to do with Kimmel's theory of Self-Made Men trying to reclaim their lost manhood as they do with "real" art. "The identification of phantasy is always an attempt to avoid one's own suffering," Auden concludes; "the identification of art is a compelled sharing in the suffering of another." But Auden does make a concession: "It is possible, however," he offers, "that an analysis of the detective story, i.e., of the kind of detective story I enjoy, may throw light, not only on its magical function, but also, by contrast, on the function of art."

While I was feeling terrified about K's loss of vision and nervous as hell about my ability to commit to the level of care El needed, I experienced writer's block. But it wasn't just writer's block—it was full on artist's block. I couldn't create anything. Even when I wasn't writing in the past, I always spent time taking photographs, making collages, wiring bonsai trees—I even count arranging the bulbs in our front landscaping so flowers bloom in every season as creative work. But my creativity had been leveled by the tidal wave of responsibility-altering changes that defined my life in West Virginia.

K was aware of the malaise I was experiencing in my creativity, and she wanted to remind me that I would be the same person I had always been, still the kid who went to college to study visual art. That version of me felt like a stranger now that I was encumbered with a spouse and a baby and a dog and a job and a house payment. The identity I'd forged prior to being a husband and a father didn't fit me anymore. I needed to change my perspective and remake myself, but I needed help to do it.

K bought me a wall-sized blank canvas for my birthday to inspire me. It was a thoughtful metaphor, but it still left me with a practical problem: what do I with it? Buy a beret and a palette and paint a landscape? Paint it a field of blue and title it *Blue*? Hang it in El's nursery? I lugged the canvas to our attic and leaned it against the wall in my "art corner," where I kept all the boxes of my art supplies, piles of portfolios filled with work from art school, and a bricolage of artful objects—computer motherboards, antique wrenches, broken cameras—I occasionally gathered in fits of inspiration for projects I never started.

The canvas. Enormous and blank. Beautiful but dangerous. And I have never been much of a painter. My approach to art always skewed conceptual. I view life in all its devastating amazingness as performance art—especially the everyday experiences that we don't assign much value to. Those moments when we just do, and don't think—buying gas or coffee, walking or driving to work, sleeping or eating—I can't stop documenting those experiences, filling folders with grocery receipts and clothing tags, for-sale stickers and complementary bookmarks born of mundane encounters with the material world.

I can have a transcendent moment looking at the time stamp on an ATM receipt. I mean, what the fuck! To be alive and withdrawing money and not thinking anything of it! It all matters so much—the life we overlook as we are living it and the traces we leave that prove it—sometimes I think a key to empathy lies there no matter how different we think we are. It makes my heart bulge, and I recognize that young man from art school has left his trace within me.

The closest I ever came to making art out of ATM receipts was when I lobbied my college friends for months that we should drop out of school, move to New York City, and buy a house. We could make the exterior and interior walls glass, and when it was finished, we would just live in it. That was it. That was the plan. I wanted to invite people into our home like it was an art museum. Or like a live-action anthropological exhibit. It would be free (donations encouraged but not required), and people could walk through our house whenever they wanted. The whole space would be open for their perusal and investigation, like a real world version of the Sims, or like a next-level version of MTV's *Real World*, seven strangers picked to live in a house but the camera never stops rolling, the tape is never edited, and I would always be on display and observable at all times in all of my mundane glory. Our "Art House" would be like Warhol's factory, only the opposite. It would not be exclusive. It would just be a normal house where you might stop by and catch me two bottles of wine in and roaring about radical politics or space–time theory, or in my robe making breakfast and listening to a scratchy classical record, or playing video games, or snoring, but the point was I would always be there; all of us would be there with nothing left to hide.

I imagined that people would be intrigued at first, then probably ignore us for a long stretch of time, but at some point our Art House would become important because we had never left, never hung curtains, even when everyone stopped looking and forgot about us, and that's when we would have made it.

I still think it would have worked, especially by now: we'd be over a decade in, still just living like always, open and available.

My friends obviously didn't go for it, and I was too chickenshit to build a glass house in New York by myself.

Not to mention I had no money or connections.

Not to mention my enrollment as an art major in my home-town college inaugurated my failure to live the artist's life, choosing it over a scholarship offer to study art at Pratt—my best chance at the big lights and big stage of the Big Apple—because I was intimidated and afraid.

Not to mention, I was eighteen and didn't want to move so far away from family or that I had a girlfriend who was a year behind me in high school and was already making concessions for the people who supported me emotionally, already know-ing I needed them more than I wanted to believe.

I dropped out of college after a year and a half. I was too immature at nineteen to be making choices about my life and living on my own, and I got into drugs and drinking as a way to rationalize the failure I could see awaiting me in the future, as I had no practical career in mind and my loans were already mounting.

I couldn't see how to become the kind of artist I wanted to be without someone's help.

Frank Streets slammed on his brakes in an indistinguishable stretch of road. He took a quick right onto a single-lane dirt street pocked with deep holes that wound steeply uphill. When we crested the hill, there was a sagging, trailer-sized house perched above us on our left and a severe concrete staircase leading up to its rickety deck.

"That place doesn't look like it's standing too well," I said and chuckled uncomfortably.

"Doesn't look like there could be anyone there," Jim added breathily. "Holy Toledo." The roof was more than falling in on itself, the ragged edge of shingles around the concavity that engulfed half of the roof looked sharp, like the seashells that gather in rifts at the edge of the tide as they wait for the next wave to smooth them into the sea. The house was shrouded in a patchwork of blue tarps that were stretched to their sinewy limits by the stagnant water that pooled in them, pressing down into the home below. Several threadbare sections of tarp flapped in the wind.

"I'm gonna run up and see if she's in there." Frank Streets unbuckled, and we all stared warily at the house. I couldn't imagine anyone living in it.

The house looked like it had been dropped from the sky and buckled upon impact. It reminded me of an essay I'd read by Lia Purpura about her friend who purchases condemned houses, lifts them into the sky via cranes and helicopters, and then photographs them as they plummet and impact the ground.

Purpura says his intent isn't to literalize a metaphor for the destruction of the family, nor is it a comment on the safety and stability a house represents, the demolition of that myth. I'm not so sure.

Purpura quotes the artist as saying, "the process was never intended to be a concern for the viewer."

But I'm suspicious of the sanctity of a house falling from the sky. I need to believe art also thrived in it before, in the unposed lives that scurried through it when it was solidly on the ground, filled with a family going about their business of sleeping and eating and shitting and laughing and crying and screaming, dreaming they could drop whatever they wanted from the sky as long as they did it together, and not worry if it was good art or bad art or if anyone cared.

"It is more like returning to an old house whose floors are strewn with litter and whose rooms are stacked full of cookie jars and photo albums and faded letters," Sonja Livingston writes of her process as a writer. "I enter that house and begin to wade through it all, picking things up one at a time, examining them—sometimes with wonder or sadness or even regret—but looking closely, taking my time and making note of things before setting them into their proper places and moving on."

And I can make a house fall from the sky in about a minute

with Photoshop. I did learn something in art school, after all.

To remove the messy process of living from art and only share the sterile version you want people to believe is too manipulative to be authentic. It's just too clean to be true.

How does someone move from the routines of an ordinary life to those required to drop a house from the sky, from sleeping and eating and drinking coffee and checking Twitter and changing diapers and all the rest of it to making art for art's sake? If I was that artist, how would I rectify the guilt I felt every time I left home while K and El were still eating breakfast to go to a site with a helicopter and a crane and a house emptied of furniture, without cabinets full of table settings, without pantries jangling with canned goods, with no crumbs that need to be vacuumed, with no toys that need to be picked up, just to drop it from the sky and not share that process with anyone? How can a man dropping a house from the sky to destroy it not become a metaphor for his crisis of masculinity?

Auden explains the appeal of detective fiction by discussing other genres of escapist stories that he has no interest in—namely love stories with happy endings. "I cannot answer that I have no phantasies of being handsome and loved and rich, because of course I have," Auden admits. "No, I can only say that I am too conscious of the absurdity and evil of such wishes to enjoy seeing them reflected in print."

Like most men, Auden can resist—or at least subdue—his desires for fame, fortune, and good looks. But his dilemma is that he cannot eliminate these fantasies entirely, and necessarily spends his life resisting them. This dialectic between ethical behavior in the face of hedonistic desires is an internal conflict most if not all men can empathize with. "It is the fact that I have them which makes me feel guilty," Auden explains, "so that instead of dreaming about indulging my desires, I dream about the removal of the guilt which I feel at their existence."

Auden writes that a reader of detective stories suffers from an acute sense of sin, feeling the ethical responsibility held in each decision he makes in his life. "From the point of view of ethics," Auden rationalizes, "desires and acts are good or bad, and I must choose the good and reject the bad." But before the choice is made, the I floats in a state of ethical neutrality. It is only in making a choice at all that the outcome of that choice can be deemed good or bad, only in that outcome that someone can be judged as good or bad for having made the choice he did. "To have a sense of sin means to feel guilty at there being an ethical choice to make," Auden admits, "a guilt which, however 'good' I may become, remains unchanged."

"What's the name we're looking for?" Jim asked, still eyeing the devastated structure of the house on the hill.

"Mariela," Frank Streets blurted and jumped out of the Escape. Jim and I watched as he walked across the dirt road to the steep cement stairway that led to the front porch.

"Careful on the steps, Frank," Jim said sarcastically to himself. "That should've been condemned twenty years ago."

We watched with concern as Frank Streets crept up the staircase.

"Those aren't flowers, Frank," Jim quipped as Frank Streets took a look at the weeds growing along the bank and encroaching on the cracked cement of the steps. "That's not landscaping."

Once at the top, Frank Streets had to maneuver around several weather-faded children's toys and a haphazard pile of tools to get to the door. He knocked, and a minute passed before an obese woman in a loose-fitting T-shirt and sweatpants answered the door.

"Must be the right place," Jim snapped. "And she sure fits the scene. Isn't that exactly what you expected to walk out the door?"

I laughed dutifully. We watched as the woman momentarily disappeared back inside, leaving the door open. Frank Streets stood firm; it looked like he was saying something vociferously into the house, his posture wide, fists clenched at his side, his jaw flapping rapidly like a caricature of someone shouting to someone far away. The woman reappeared, shouting over her shoulder as she walked out onto the deck and slammed the door behind her. She stretched her arms over her head and rubbed her forehead like she was just waking up.

"That's right, just scratch your belly, hanging out of your shirt," Jim cracked.

"So, you've been working on the case of the sheriff, too?" I asked nervously.

"Oh, yeah." Jim nodded his head deliberately.

"I bet that's been keeping you busy."

"Very." His eyes never strayed from Frank Streets. "Keeps you busy, keeps you disgusted, keeps you mad."

"I bet," I interrupted. I wanted to sound like I knew everything about the case, even though I didn't. "I've been keeping up with it in talking with Frank Streets and reading a ton online."

Just as I was about to mention Blue Gray Ghost's allusion to more girls with accusations against the sheriff to try to read his reaction, Frank Streets began to walk down the steps with the woman following closely behind.

"Looks like they're coming down to the vehicle. That means I'll have to climb back there with you, and probably stay there the rest of the day. I don't wanna sit back in that seat after she's been there."

The woman hiked up her purple polka-dotted pajama pants as she crossed the dirt road toward us. She wasn't wearing any shoes. My eyes skipped quickly to the door of the house as it opened again. A small boy with a thatch of blond hair emerged and warily eyed the Escape parked in front of his home. He was no more than four years old. He hung in the doorway for a minute before moseying slowly out onto the deck, ignoring the piles of toys and junk as he kept his eyes glued on Frank Streets and the woman. His mother.

"My boyfriend was freaking out," the woman said as she opened the door and hoisted herself into the passenger seat.

"I heard him," Frank Streets responded toughly. "Wasn't sure if I'd have to shoot him or something." He didn't laugh.

"No," she said loudly, but not in a fearful way. "He's just freaking out on me."

"What was he saying? I heard him yelling," Frank Streets asked.

"He said, 'Who are they? What do they want?'" the woman mimicked in a raspy voice.

"Heard that." Frank Streets's anger over the confrontation with the boyfriend manifested in how aggressively he flipped through his notebook. Jim and I exchanged uncomfortable glances in the backseat as Frank Streets took some notes.

The woman didn't seem nervous at all about sitting in the cab of this vehicle with three men somehow associated with an investigation of a murdered baby. I watched as the boy hesitantly shuffled toward the top of the steps, his gaze shifting slowly from his feet to the vehicle that his mom was just escorted into.

"The statement you gave the prosecution says you lived in the Jane Lew Apartments next door to Julie Mick, is that correct?"

"Yes."

"It has you saying that the day before the baby's death you made a comment that you saw her outside smoking and he was just in there screaming."

Mariela nodded confidently. "She said he wasn't feeling good."

"But your comment was that it sounded like more," Frank Streets implored.

"Like it was hurt, yeah. Consistent for a little, then he just stopped."

"Did you ever see Christopher Sheppard there?"

"Yeah, but Chris only come down a few times. They would usually go up to his mom's in Hepzibah. I'm not allowed there 'cause his mama can't stand me," she added without a flicker of humor.

"Why's that?"

"When we first met, me and Chris—"

"Did you date him?" Frank Streets interrupted.

"No, no, no," she said, her voice textured like a rock quarry. "Nuh-uh. He was a little cocky for me." Jim squirmed next to me.

"What about a guy named Rodney Weaver. They call him Skinny. Have you ever heard of him?"

"Yes," Mariela said. "He's sort of, kind of, my cousin." Jim and I looked at each other instinctually. Jim raised his eyebrow, and then turned to look back out the window. The little boy had made his way down to the street. He was prodding at some dirt along the side of the bank with a stick he had pulled out of the overgrowth. He wore oversized work boots, and his blue jeans had large holes in both knees despite being a size that he might not grow into for several years. He looked up at us, and I sensed concern in the hard line of his mouth, the squint of his eyes.

"Skinny dated her for a little while prior to Chris," Frank Streets stated.

"No," Mariela protested, "he stayed there a couple times, but they didn't date." Meaning, they fucked, but nothing more.

"What about Skinny," Frank Streets pressed. "Could he have abused that baby in any way shape or form?"

"No. I would trust my kids' lives in his hands." She sounded sincere, but I couldn't help but look at the boy staring down at us and think of El, how vulnerable children are and how violent men can be.

"Okay. Any other guys she might have been involved with?"

"There was this guy once, I don't know his first name. I know he has kinda long red hair and she met him at the bar.

What was his name . . ." Mariela trailed off. Frank Streets stared hard at her. This was a person he hadn't heard of yet.

"When was this?" he demanded.

"Me, her, Chris, and Skinny, we went to a bar out in Lost Creek, and she met up with the redheaded guy there and he made her cry, then she took us home, then she left me at another bar in Jane Lew and I guess went back to that guy's house."

"And this was at the time she was seeing Chris?" Frank Streets asked interestedly.

"Yes."

"Did she ever bring that guy home to her apartment?"

"No. That was the first and last time I'd ever even seen that guy. I was with some guy with a baseball hat that night. I thought his name was Lucky, but it might have been Bucky." Mariela looked sheepish for the first time, but hardly girlish.

"Bucky and Lucky, huh." Frank Streets was visibly agitated with Mariela, and he adjusted his weight purposefully in his seat. "Julie had a lot of issues with guys. Her low self-esteem, she felt degraded, whatever. Could it be possible that if she was getting close to a guy and getting ready to settle down, if they touched that child," Frank Streets smacked his hands together hard, the crack loud enough to make me jump, "that she could overlook that?"

"It could be possible," Mariela nodded. She was the only one in the vehicle who didn't seem jarred by Frank Streets's loud clap. "I know from my own experience, you always think you can change them." I looked over at Jim, but he didn't look back. He stared deliberately out the window at the little boy as he whacked his stick against an electric meter nestled crookedly along the side of the road.

"Do you know where Pick lives?"

"Yeah, the street just to the left of the four-way in Lost Creek. There's a wheelchair place and a burned-out trailer. She drives a gray Cherokee and parks it in front of her place. You'll see it." She smiled kindly.

"Alright then, thanks for your time," Frank Streets said

abruptly. "We'll be in touch with you if there's anything else we need."

"I really do hope that if someone else is involved, that they get what they deserve," Mariela said.

"Me too." Frank Streets's face was buried in his folio.

"Alright, thank you," Mariela shouted with what felt like too much enthusiasm given the scope of the conversation. She exited the car and walked briskly over to the steps, her pajamas hiked up at to her thighs.

"Now get the hell out of my car," Frank Streets growled under his breath as soon as the door had closed behind her. "Before I shoot your boyfriend." He was fuming. I'd never seen him like this before.

The little boy didn't react to Mariela reappearing from inside the strange vehicle; I assumed he would be relieved to see his mom reemerge, run over wildly to her, innocently, his arms wide, his face untethered in a way that betrayed how difficult it is to hold it all in sometimes. But he didn't. He watched her, holding his stick prone by the electrical meter while she scuttled past him up the steps. I couldn't tell from his reaction if he even acknowledged him. Maybe Mariela wasn't his mother. Maybe she was more concerned about what her boyfriend would do when she returned to the house.

"She got that name wrong. About that boy she was with that night—Bucky, Lucky—I bet he hasn't been called that since," Jim quipped. "I think it was Un-Lucky."

"I agree." Frank Streets said definitively. "You coming up?"

"Not for a while. Probably bugs crawling on that seat." I eyed the seat warily. "I don't picture the inside looking like a mansion with the outside looking like it does," Jim prodded.

"She said they were remodeling." Frank Streets didn't laugh.

"The only way to remodel that place is with a can of gasoline and a match," Jim added. "Did you see the extension cord running to the camper across the street?" I looked up quickly and saw a fluorescent orange extension cord running from just by the electrical meter to across the dirt road and disappearing in the tall grass. A few hundred feet down the hill there was a rusted hull of a trailer. I had been too distracted by the little boy to notice it. "Half of them were probably living there too." Frank Streets nodded disinterestedly. The boy cast one more look our way and then trudged stoically up the steps, and I still can't get him out of my head.

We came to an empty four-way stop. Indistinguishable brick buildings hunkered around the intersection with windows still fogged with winter grime. I stole a glance at the sun patch on the seat next to me, then looked up at Frank Streets, who sat staring into the empty intersection. "We're in Lost Creek," Frank Streets announced rhetorically.

"Should be a wheelchair place," Jim said.

"There it is," Frank Streets said. I had wondered before where wheelchairs are made. Any specialized chairs, really, like barber chairs or dentist chairs. And here, in Lost Creek, West Virginia, of all places, I found my answer.

We took a left and bucked over a large pothole, turning down a dirt alleyway overgrown with Queen Anne's lace. We were looking for the remnants of a trailer that had recently burned down.

"The trailer, there on the right. And there's the gray Cherokee like Mariela said," Jim chirped.

Pick's house was only larger than a trailer thanks to the weathered and unpainted wooden porch attached to the front. Maybe it wasn't attached but propped. A graying wooden swing hung on the end just above a blue lawn tractor that was parked on an angle in the front yard, the wheels sunk a foot down in mud.

"Pick lives here, huh?" Frank Streets said and put the Escape in park. "This is our last stop for the day. Let's see what she has to say." He exhaled skeptically and climbed out. Jim and I stayed in the vehicle and watched him walk carefully up the front steps of the porch, each one visibly sagging under his weight.

"Pick was with the mother on the day of the death," Jim punctuated each word deliberately. "Pick supposedly had left her apartment to go to a friend's house to get a refrigerator for another friend. The friend with the refrigerator said the mother showed up that morning by herself; the two of them couldn't load the refrigerator, so the mother left, said she was gonna come back with this Pick and Fee everyone's talking about." Jim and I watched Frank Streets knock heavily on the door.

Pick's door opened slightly, and Frank Streets immediately started jawing. The woman that answered was petite, wearing short-cut sweat shorts and a red tank top.

"Farrah Fawcett hair," Jim said. "Feathered back."

Frank Streets and the young woman walked over and sat down on the porch swing. "I don't know if that thing will hold the two of you, Frank," Jim quipped to himself with a hint of sincerity. He kept his eyes on Frank Streets and the girl. "Pick was friends with the mother," he continued. "Hung around with her and Sheppard. She might know if the mother was mistreating the child before."

We watched Frank Streets talk to Farrah Fawcett, her arms crossed as she leaned against the doorframe, one leg elbowed outward, the bottom of its bare foot rubbing slowly up and down along the inside of the other leg.

"It's amazing how many people, when you walk in and start talking to them like that don't even ask you who you are," Jim thought aloud. "Who are you? What do you want? Not many people ask." Jim rolled down his window and slouched. I followed his cue and rolled my window down.

"I've been shocked by that, too. People just started pouring their guts out to us, without any need to confirm who we are or what we really want." They were so trusting, so confident, so immediately open and available, even if it was simply because they assumed we were cops.

"You can buy a badge at Family Dollar for ninety-nine

cents, you know?" Jim whispered out of the side of his mouth.
"It's how you approach people, if you look nervous and hesitant, they're gonna say, 'Who is this guy?' And Frank puts on
a different persona when he's talking to people, too, if you
notice, his attitude will change, his mood will change, he'll get
more forceful and direct."

Jim's understanding of Frank Streets's method reminded me
of Auden's point that the detective's job is to vet each character within the dialectic of innocence and guilt that directs
the detective story, "to restore the state of grace in which the
aesthetic and the ethical are as one."

He delineates the differences between professional and
amateur detectives by outlining the requirement each has for
solving the mystery of the crime. For Auden, the professional
detective is aesthetically uninteresting, but that's unimportant
to the reader because he is a representative of the ethical. In
being the representative of the ethical state of grace to which
the narrative is destined to conclude, the professional detective
sidesteps any need for motive for investigating the crime. He
investigates the case because he is an agent of pure justice, and
there was a crime, and therefore the truth must be revealed.
Justice must be served, and investigation is just what he does
because it is the logical path toward uncovering truth. There is
no personal desire for this professional detective. No internal
conflict. his authority is righteous without question, and I cannot relate to that.

I thought about the influence authority has over people,
whether perceived or real. When Frank Streets and Jim and I
let the people we confronted assume we were police detectives,
they told us everything when they didn't have to. They trusted
us. Or, they feared us.

"Are there more girls out there that are going to claim that
Hawkins had sex with them?" Blue Gray Ghost speculates
in another post on his blog. "Well I can't name anyone by
name," he continues, "but I will say I know of another and
yet that poor girl has refused to come forward out of fear of

retribution. Will the girl I have heard from come forward or will she continue to hide in the shadows out of fear?" Blue Gray Ghost laments. "Fear should never be a tool to be used by one individual against another."

Auden says that unlike the professional detective like Sherlock Holmes or Father Brown in the whodunits he prefers, the amateur detective—the private investigator—is not an agent of justice. He is an exceptional individual with some aesthetic interest—as long as it does not fully betray the ethical standards required to pursue the truth objectively. The amateur detective, however, may need to reveal a motive for pursuing the cases they are interested in.

In either case, Auden argues, the detective in a story must not be influenced by personal or professional desires along the way, otherwise his ability to maintain a level of disinterest in his pursuit of justice is compromised. If the detective is invested in the outcome of the case he is working on—if he desires a certain truth, or a payoff contingent on which version of truth is revealed—it would sully the sanctity of the very work he is prescribed to complete. It might even lead someone to coerce or repress certain information.

And I was implicated in the work Frank Streets was prescribed to complete. Didn't my own authority as a writer demand the same trust from Frank Streets and Jim, from all the people I had been meeting and talking to and observing? But Frank Streets, Jim, and I weren't police. I wasn't a detective, barely a writer in a tangible way: I had nothing to prove that I was, other than what people assumed based on the way I presented myself: I was an amateur posing with the aesthetic of a professional, trying to fake it till I make it, by god.

"I'm a writer," I'd tell them, even though I had no book. But I was documenting my observations of these very real people in this very real place at this very real time, even if a reality-show storyline never emerged from it. So what if it just remained one of the vast majority of boring investigations of the world that don't amount to anything, the literary equivalent of sitting in a truck all day and staring at a driveway. Would that make it less meaningful? Would it make the people revealed in the process less important?

Jim's attention turned to another female who had arrived at the house. She was much bulkier than the girl on the swing. A large white T-shirt hugged her midsection close while hanging loosely from her sloped shoulders, the sleeves extending almost to mid-forearm. She wore cutoff camouflage cargo shorts and a faded camouflage hat pulled down over her eyes. She strode up onto the porch like people in flip-flops do, wide-legged and with her feet facing outward, and went right inside the house without even looking at Frank Streets, like it was normal to see a man asking questions on her front porch. Farrah Fawcett sprung off the swing and followed her in the house, leaving Frank Streets alone. He didn't move.

Jim jumped out and strode toward the porch, pulling out and lighting a cigarette in one fluid motion, and I followed. No more than thirty seconds passed and both women reemerged. The boyish woman gripped a pack of cigarettes, lit one up, and sat down roughly on the swing next to Frank Streets, the chains creaking beneath their combined mass. Jim held the drag of his cigarette a beat longer, exhaling only after they didn't crash to the ground. Farrah Fawcett sat quickly in the plastic lawn chair on other side of the porch, facing the swing, and folded both legs under herself with surprising ease.

The way the scene was arranged from where Jim and I loitered at the bottom of the steps gave the impression that I was watching an off-off-Broadway production. The set was modest but fitting, the cast small but well selected. I sat down on the front porch step and listened.

"I went to prison and talked to Sheppard, and I said all these reports I got, why don't you show any remorse? And he said, 'Well, if I'm driving down the road and your cat comes into the road and I hit your cat, you're gonna have remorse but I'm not, it's nothing to me. So, he's comparing a baby to a cat? So, I looked at him and said, 'You are one stupid son of a bitch,' and that's exactly what I said." Frank Streets's stare was aimed directly at the stocky woman on the swing next to him, who I assumed was Pick, based on the description Mariela had provided. His head swiveled to Farrah Fawcett: Fee.

"Not stupid, it's kind of sickening." Fee crossed her arms, her face puckering like it was pulled from within.

Frank Streets talked with Pick and Fee briefly about their relationships with Julie before asking if they ever saw her abuse or neglect Rex.

"Oh my god, no," Fee exclaimed, her hand fluttering to her neck. Pick nodded stoically in agreement, as she and Frank Streets creaked back and forth, each with the foot tip touching the ground like ballerinas in pointe. It was subtle, the way one or both pushed them, but their movement wasn't a result of wind or shifting body weight. It was oddly relaxing to watch, despite Pick's stiffness and stare fixed somewhere on the floorboards at the middle of the set, betraying her discomfort with the conversation.

Fee, on the other hand, was relaxed and conversational. Giddy even, fidgeting naturally in the lawn chair, tucking and untucking her feet under herself in a variety of positions.

"Never see her leave the child unattended?"

"Never around here," Fee said simply while Pick took a drag of her cigarette.

Frank Streets raised his voice: "I mean literally with nobody around?"

"Oh, no," Fee squealed, and Pick mumbled in agreement.

"That's what the rumor is around the complex." Frank Streets paused, ushering silence among the actors through his shifting gaze. "That she would just take off and the baby would be there all by itself."

Pick and Fee shook their heads again. I had an abrupt thump of fear at the thought of leaving El unattended. I've canceled trips with friends and bowed out of professional obligations because I don't want to leave him, even when K is there, because I feel irresponsible if I choose myself over him, even for worthy reasons. I never want him to look at me and conclude I was absent, think that I cared about myself more than him.

Frank Streets pressed about the day Rex was murdered. Pick narrated the story about how she woke up early that day because she had to work — she's a flagger for construction on state roads — and how she was calling Julie that morning because she had promised to bring Pick a refrigerator from a friend's house. Julie stalled by several hours, feeding Pick a litany of excuses for why she couldn't bring the refrigerator, blaming it on everything from accidentally falling back asleep to being on her period. When Julie finally got the refrigerator, she brought it to Pick's house and hung out for a while. She didn't have Rex with her. Julie told Pick that she'd left him with Sheppard because "he didn't want to be by himself" and had persuaded her to leave the baby with him.

Pick said that when she had to leave for work, she and Julie left together and went to the store to buy cigarettes. She said she gave Julie a hydrocodone at the store and watched her take it there in front of her.

"I kept trying to get ahold of her that day but never could," Pick said in a gravelly voice that cracked like someone who prefers not to talk. She pulled hard on her cigarette. "Four or five in the morning, I got a phone call telling me the baby had died." She hesitated for a moment, weighing what to say next. "Julie supposedly shot Chris up with a subbie tab and left the baby with him. She told me she helped him shoot up," Pick said, her hand and voice shaking. "But she only told me that a long time after everything had happened."

Frank Streets locked eyes with Jim and held his gaze. "Here's my thing," he said with a touch of anger in his voice. "If Julie's involved, if somebody else is involved, that baby needs justice. Leave Sheppard locked up, where his ass belongs, but somebody else is involved because of the prior broken ribs that were mending. So that baby was abused several months prior to his death." Frank Streets glowered at the actors on set.

Frank Streets told Pick and Fee a story about a woman he recently interviewed who would sometimes watch Julie's baby. The woman said she had taken to the baby as if he were one of her grandchildren, and that Rex was the happiest little baby. But she had told him that when she would pick the baby up he would wince and cry out.

"When she told Julie that she should take the baby to the doctor, Julie never went back to her house," Frank Streets said with a sneer.

"I told her to take him to the doctor many a times," Pick growled and pulled another cigarette from her pack, her lips pursed. "She always said they already did."

"She never took the baby to the doctor?" Fee asked warily, her mouth agape as she looked at Pick. Frank Streets frowned and shook his head.

"Then she's involved," Pick said, sighing heavily and shaking her head.

"But how?" Frank Streets demanded through clenched teeth. He could sense this was the moment when stories are puzzled together, and he pressed for it.

"I can't see her abusing her baby, but maybe she changed when she got with Chris," Pick said contemplatively.

"I think if she knew anything then she hid it because she didn't want anybody to know about him," Fee thought aloud.

"She was on drugs?" Frank Streets asked bluntly.

"I never saw her do anything," Fee began innocently before Pick interrupted her.

"We didn't know she was shooting that boy up until the detective told me. That's the honest truth."

"The boy or the baby?" Frank Streets asked urgently, leaning forward on the swing. The actors froze in place, the swing static in a position that according to the laws of physics it couldn't possibly be, and I held my breath, my heart still in my throat.

"Not the baby, Chris." Pick said dismissively. "But remember we heard that Chris gave that baby a subbie or something? Half or a quarter of a subbie tab, to keep him from crying while Julie was there."

"So, in other words, if the baby had drugs in its system, there's another reason she wouldn't want to take it to the doctor." Frank Streets stared daggers at Jim. Pick was visibly emotional, her hand shaking as she slowly moved her cigarette to her mouth.

"If they would've went to the doctor." Fee's voice broke as she looked to the floor.

"That baby might still be alive," Frank Streets completed her thought. "That child might not be lying under the ground right now because CPS would've stepped in and taken the child out of there."

"Pick and I tried to get her to give us that baby, to raise him, so she could do whatever she wanted." As a look of deep pain overtook Fee, an image of a small boy wearing ripped jeans and oversized work boots and brandishing a stick materialized in my mind. I zoomed in on his face, a crease running between eyes rimmed with apprehension, a firm lower lip earned by being alone too often. I pictured Pick and Fee looking at each other with clear intentions, reorienting their priorities with such ease as they walked to him and scooped him up, his legs dangling freely, the stick dropping from his grip as they carried him onto the porch and toward the door. And Pick's trailer suddenly looked different; it was warm and loving, ramshackle but sturdy enough. It was a home, and they would be good parents.

"We tried," Fee repeated to herself.

Frank Streets pulled up next to my car in the back of the Walmart parking lot. The RV and trailer were gone, as were most of the other vehicles. It was 4:34 pm.

As I hopped out of the Escape, Frank Streets rolled down his window and smirked.

"Hey, Steve? Your car's kind of cute, but it looks like you picked it too soon."

"You said it was blue," Jim chimed in, "but that looks more purple than blue."

"What's your wife drive?" Frank Streets bellowed, and I could tell that it was a rhetorical question. Technically, the car belonged to both of us; it was the first K and I had bought together, and both of our names were on the title. I giggled and rolled my eyes dramatically.

As I circled to my door, Jim catcalled, "You could get a plate on the back of it that says 'plum crazy.'"

"Yeah, and bedazzle it with some sequins, right?" I grinned and stood tall.

"There you go!" he replied with a pleased smile.

I turned to face Frank Streets. "Can I catch up with you in your office sometime soon, to follow up on this case?" I asked confidently. "Plus, to talk about what you have going on with the sheriff," I added quickly. We hadn't discussed it much as the day went on, but I wanted Frank Streets to know what story I was really after. I wasn't through with him just yet, and I had a feeling he wasn't through with me either; as a writer, I wielded an important power for him. I was a path to an audience that extended beyond the isolated hollows and country roads of West Virginia; I was a means for him to realize the kind of man he imagined himself to be. We were linked in that way.

"Give me a call," he said with faux exasperation, rolled up his window, and accelerated away.

In an interview with Terry Gross on *Fresh Air*, Jonathan Franzen was asked about his decision to not have kids. He said there was a point when he was feeling lost and alone, "like this kind of inert figure floating toward old age" while writing what would become his novel *Freedom*. He told Gross that he felt a need to have some kids, and he planned to adopt orphaned Iraqi refugees "because it was just too much pressure to just be a writer."

Franzen's comments ignited ridicule over his position of privilege as a white man and his self-serving and naive perspective on the responsibility of parenthood. But what sticks out to me is how he thinks life as a parent is "easier than writing a book," and that it would provide a flavor of satisfaction and sense of worth akin to what he wasn't getting from his life as writer.

"I was brought to my senses by my *New Yorker* editor," Franzen continued, "who said 'many people can become good parents; not many people can write novels like yours.' So, what I would've lost [in having kids] was an opportunity to really devote myself to digging ever deeper in my books."

To be fair, he did say he thought he would've become "a different kind of person, and maybe a better person" if he'd gone through with adopting kids. But Franzen's point about "losing the opportunity to really devote himself" to "digging ever deeper in my books," is his way of saying, "If I had kids, my writing wouldn't be as good."

Because writing is divine and parenting is mundane, and the latter would pull the former into its middling maw.

"The image of the artist as a solitary genius—so noble, so enviable, so pleasant an object of aspiration and projection—has kept its hold on the collective imagination," William Deresiewicz writes. "'He's an artist,' we'll say in tones of reverence . . . meaning someone who appears to dwell upon a higher plane. Vision, inspiration, mysterious gifts as from above: such are some of the associations that continue to adorn the word."

"The priest departs," said Whitman, "the divine literatus comes." Whitman is one of my writer–heroes, and I aspire to yawp like him, to strive toward authentic openness, to have my heart and mind bulge forth to the future, to have my procreant urge souse readers with my perspective on the kosmos, but I am no priest, and with my entanglements with K and El, I am by no measure solitary.

But Whitman was just another man hung up on his penis, too. One weekend in graduate school I attended a conference focused solely on Whitman, and one presenter displayed what looked like two identical versions of the frontispiece for the 1855 *Leaves of Grass*, with one notable difference: the later version had a more heavily shadowed crease on the poet's pants that emphasizes his, ahem, procreant urge. This proto-Photoshopped frontispiece is of course the version that Whitman chose to feature in his book, an example that even the bard of American manliness felt the need to amplify his manhood in what amounts to sending an unsolicited dick pic to his dear readers.

I have been imprinted with this belief about artists, making it easy for me to see parenthood as Franzen and his *New Yorker* editor pal do: it signals the death of the writer. The moment of El's birth was the clock striking high noon in the sepia-toned ghost town of my identity. There I am and there I am, Stephen the Writer and Steve the Family Man, spinning on my heels and drawing, this life ain't big enough for the both of me, because that is what I had been taught to believe.

At the time K and I found out she was pregnant, I hadn't published anything. I had sent my writing places, but only occasionally, and the rejection letter would arrive within three to six months. It wasn't that I didn't like the rejection. In some ways, it was the most satisfying part of the process. I felt a thrill when an envelope would arrive in my mailbox addressed to me and penned in my own handwriting. I'd rip it open and read the curt "Dear Writer" note it contained, most of which were only printed on a postcard to save money and paper. I loved the idea that I was sending myself letters that I would get a few months later announcing my failure to myself. I began submitting my work more often, sending it to more prestigious magazines to ensure those rejection letters I sent myself kept arriving. When I recognized one of those precious

"Dear Writer" letters, I would take it to the attic and paste the note and the envelope to my enormous birthday canvas with a liberal glob of matte medium unearthed from my art corner.

"Did you know Sylvia Plath was rejected hundreds of times before she published *The Bell Jar*?" K said as she warily eyed my collage of rejections as they bloomed on my canvas.

"Yeah, and you know how her story ends, right?" I joked, but I got her drift. But the rejections didn't bother me, because I was inspired again. By giving me the enormous canvas and the freedom to do whatever I wanted with it, K helped me overcome my artist's block. I could feel how common and necessary failure is in both art and life—how together those failures can make a path to empathy—and if I could transform my failures into a muse, I just might reinvent myself.

Following in the tradition of escapist books featuring the exploits of cowboys and Indians on the vanished frontier, the detective story took hold of the Self-Made Man's imagination in the 1930s and soared in popularity through the middle of the century. But the detectives embraced by American men received a makeover from the genteel and ethical types in houndstooth jackets native to Auden's whodunits. Kimmel describes these hard-boiled detectives as "adventurous and cold men who stalked the urban jungle, a world where women were either seductive vixens enticing men to their doom or angelic innocents needing their help (but never their marital commitment)": a fantasy tailored to Self-Made Men who were feeling emasculated as they worked at home and took care of children, burdened by their conformity to a domestic sphere they never intended to be a part of.

"The detectives of the hard-boiled school," Auden writes, "are motivated by avarice or ambition and might just as well be murderers." These antiheroes defied the formulaic character requirements of Auden's murder-mysteries, and in doing so, dismantled the clean purity of ethics held in the dialectic between innocence and guilt. Authors like Dashiell Hammett and Raymond Chandler brought dark, unsentimental realism to the detective story for the first time, and each of their stories unfolds in a milieu of relative criminality where the most shrewd, ruthless, and enterprising come out on top. But every single one ends on the bottom eventually. There is no hope to restore the narrative to an ethical state of grace in "The Great Wrong Place," as Auden calls the world of hard-boiled detective stories. It never existed in the first place.

At their core, the hard-boiled story is not really interested in detective stories, but sobering investigations of the dark corners of the American male psyche. For Auden, these are "depressing" books that "should be read and judged, not as escape literature, but as works of art."

When I wasn't trying to get El to eat or sleep or stop crying and took a break from the backlog of student papers that I needed to grade, I "conducted research" by reading and watching detective novels and movies from a long list compiled by my friend Ben, a self-described fanboy of the genre. Their formulaic moves were reassuring when I felt about as secure as a moving truck parked on an incline with a faulty emergency break.

But I am not Auden. I hate the game Clue, and I am distrustful of sanitized solutions to complex problems. Maybe it's a generational thing—or an American thing—or a guy thing—but I'll always take a detective like Sam Spade over a gentleman like Sherlock Holmes, and *The Maltese Falcon* was my favorite of all the books I read. Maybe it was a product of time and place; that novel's seamy and ruthless characters, its grimy urbanscape and brutal competition to end up on top felt shaded with the same brushstrokes as the hardscrabble world of Appalachia K and I had moved into. I certainly felt depraved as I strode through the uneven streets of Morgantown, my hands jammed in my pockets while I tried to make heads or tails of my suddenly unfamiliar life as a father.

I spied on Bob Clay's office, trying to stay one step ahead of myself in case I was being followed by a private investigator I hired.

I fantasized about my escape from the smell of asphalt and coal trucks that honked along the thoroughfares in Morgantown like geese displaced by an oil spill.

I dreamed about following Frank Streets on another case, hoping for the worst.

I checked Blue Gray Ghost's blog for updates on the sheriff and found none.

I waited for someone to waltz into my office and give me a statuette to chase after, but my only visitors were students who needed help citing sources.

I pulled my chair up to the table on my back deck, lounged, and took a deep swig of my Amstel Light.

"So, wait, you went to an actual conference? For private investigators?"

"Sure did," I replied nonchalantly, working my jaw muscles and squinting. "It was a full-fledged conference, three days, presenters, a bunch of private investigators, and me." A satisfied laugh rose from the group gathered around the table and echoed into my backyard. K's and my teaching responsibilities were done for the semester and the weather was finally warm enough to be comfortable in a T-shirt as happy hour extended through sunset and into the twilight hours, the bats silently carving parabolas in the fuzzy violet sky overhead.

This deck gathering with a handful of friends from the neighborhood was our sendoff party. In just over a week, K would leave for Oaxaca, Mexico, to conduct research related to the book she was writing. It was a project building on her dissertation, in which she had followed political candidates that represented indigenous groups on the campaign trail in Ecuador. Among other things, her research involved hiking into the Amazon rainforest to hand out baby chickens to potential voters. There was an equivalently influential indigenous population in the state of Oaxaca, and she needed to follow politicians there to see if they also attempted to "buy votes" from these communities by offering them goods and services in exchange for their support at the ballots. Ultimately, she wanted to find out if the politicians held to their word and represented the interests of their marginalized constituents once elected or if they just exploited them to win office then forgot about them. It was an important book, and several editors were already interested in publishing it.

After K had settled in for a week and established her network of contacts at the university in Oaxaca, El and I would fly down to meet her for the remainder of the month. I was going because I wanted to travel to Oaxaca, but also because I had to: this was K's first attempt at field research since her eye surgery and the arrival of our baby. I wanted to support her. I needed to. I would drive when I could, keep the condo in order, make meals, but mostly be the primary caregiver for El, since she would be gone most days, and sometimes for several days at a stretch.

Being the primary parent didn't worry me. El and I were rock solid. K and I had been sharing parental responsibilities, so El and I had plenty of time to work out that I was basically Mama 2. The most daunting part was the twelve-hour international flight alone with a nine-month-old. I knew the trip would be a trial, but we could make it. I just hoped immigration wouldn't arrest me for suspected human trafficking.

The deck behind our house didn't have lights, so the only way to see when darkness fell was from the few candles in the center of the table. But that isn't entirely why I felt disconnected from the company that night. My adventures with Frank Streets had gone dormant, transforming into well-rehearsed monologues that I shared as party fodder. I tend to drink fast in social situations, and I don't ever slow down. I also tend to get sociopathic the more I drink, transforming into a performance artist for the good of the party. I hide in the spotlight, my stage makeup caked into a mask that looks like a smoothed-out version of me. But I didn't feel like myself that night, and hadn't for some time. I still drank fast like always but wasn't in the mood for performance. My anxiety about failing as a writer had metastasized into a deep blue state about being trapped by my responsibilities as a family man. Even my dog's need for me to take him for a walk felt inescapable.

"That's so funny," someone said, relishing the idea that I had attended a conference for private investigators. "You didn't have to go? You just went . . . for what?"

"I had no reason to be there other than that I decided to go," I said impassively. "I paid my registration fee and sat through a bunch of boring presentations about analyzing handwriting and using GPS thingies, stuff like that." The group chuckled like a pre-recorded laugh track. "I earned a certificate for my training in the craft of private investigation," I added gruffly. "I'll show it to you sometime." Someone audibly gasped.

What seemed to stymie people I told about my adventures in private investigation was that I had no reason to be involved with Frank Streets. It wasn't part of my job responsibilities; I wasn't getting paid for it; it didn't help me be a better adjunct faculty member or husband or father or dog owner or DIY house-fixer-upper. I had no real reason to be doing any of it, and that truth was beginning to feel more and more like something to be ashamed of.

"I even went to a bar to drink with some of the PIs," I teased and took a large swill of beer, absentmindedly tracing the grooves in the slate tiles on the table with my finger. Someone at the table clapped a single, sharp clap and leaned back, mouth agape with relative awe.

"Tell them about Frank Streets, about the first time you met him," K prompted. She knew I didn't like talking about my writing in too much detail, but she was my cheerleader, encouraging me against all odds, selflessly, just like always. I took another healthy gulp of beer and leaned back. Everyone was quiet. I took another drink. K knew that this audience— no native West Virginians among them—would get off on the perspective on Appalachia that Frank Streets gave me access to, and she just wanted me to see their reactions, to feel like what I was doing wasn't totally worthless.

I was about to launch into my rote description of the stuffed animals in Frank Streets's den when Sally interrupted me.

"Did you hear about the private investigator who was arrested? I just read about it in the paper yesterday." She paused. "Was that Frank Streets?" Everyone stopped and looked at me, the authority on private investigation in West Virginia. Frank Streets was my guy after all, as per the shtick.

Of all our friends in Morgantown, Sally and her husband, Fanboy Ben, knew me the best, and they had heard a lot about Frank Streets. I had known them even longer than K, having met them a decade earlier while we were all hiking the Appalachian Trail, each of us trying to prove something to ourselves and seeking support from each other in the process. Needless to say, Sally and Ben had heard me wax wildly about my artistic ambitions and whine about my habit for failure for hour after hour, day after day as we trudged for five months from Georgia to Maine. The others gathered around the table were neighborhood friends who knew hardly anything about me other than that I was K's husband and that I drank beer with PIs at a conference.

"No." I slouched with feigned disinterest. "Was it Frank Streets?" I added with half-hearted curiosity and the false insinuation that I somehow knew it wasn't, hiding my face behind my beer bottle. I was sober enough to get caught off guard by this news that I honestly should have known but too drunk to interrogate Sally with any sincere interest. I had to play it cool. If it was indeed Frank Streets, I didn't want to betray my distance from him to a group of people I was only casually acquainted with, who could judge me as the hack I already believed I was, all of whom were significantly less drunk than I was.

"I don't know—but I'm pretty sure it was in Barbour County; that's where he lives, right?" Sally asked innocently. She knew it was him.

"Yeah, that's where he lives," I confirmed, the chair creaking judgmentally. "But he works all over the state," I declared defensively and then kept mum, my cheeks flushed under the cover of night. I hoped that my silence was a bluff that made Sally appear to know less about Frank Streets than I did. I hardened my jaw and took long gulps of beer until the conversation moved to a hypothetical consideration of why one would hire a PI, my expression unmoved in the flickering candlelight.

In truth, I had no idea what was going on with Frank Streets. The last time we'd interacted was at the annual conference for the Private Investigation and Security Professionals of West Virginia, a few months after I'd worked with him and Jim on the investigation of Rex's murder. He told me he was still working with Fast Freddie and investigating the sheriff, and was also looking into a new case, a suspicious suicide in Clarksburg that made his eyes glimmer with intrigue. He was happy enough to have his fellow PIs see a writer following him around like a puppy at the conference, but he was uncharacteristically tight-lipped about his cases in front of them.

After that, I had lost track of Frank Streets, and I had lost my motivation to write. My life, like my art, was rudderless. I descended into minutiae as a means to cope with the uncertainty that dominated the long view. I read more detective stories. I investigated how to find literary agents, how to write a book prospectus, and how to make business cards from the PI swag I'd swiped at the conference. I sent query letters to dozens of agents, receiving two impersonal rejections and only dead air from the rest. I attended a writers conference to pitch my book idea to agents and editors, having made no appointments with anyone, ultimately spending more time avoiding the conference to drink and visit art galleries.

The one editor I did bumble into had the same reaction as the people gathered on my deck: Frank Streets was an interesting character, but they wanted to know why. Why was I obsessed with Frank Streets? Why did he matter? Why should anyone care about him, or me, or any of it? All I had was a scramble of car chases, interviews, and a knot of open-ended cases that didn't untie into anything meaningful.

I was flattened by the realization that I was more interested in the idea of the book than in actually writing it—more interested in my self-serving desire to have written a book about Frank Streets, about my inconsequential self, or any fucking book no matter what it was about as long as it was written and published, as if those two accomplishments would untether me from the litany of disappointments I'd become too acquainted with: my middling career, my stalled-out aspirations, my decidedly unsexy obligations to family. My failure to be the Self-Made Man I was unwittingly trying to be.

The inspiration to untie the knot of my time with Frank Streets—to uncover the source of the pressure I felt to be the successful man and artist that I always desired to be—had vanished like an adulterer running a red light. And lo, while I had been wallowing in self-pity and self-loathing, Frank Streets had been arrested. Sally had waltzed right onto my back deck and given me the black bird to chase that I had been waiting for, and I was about to fly two thousand miles away from it.

I woke up with a hangover the morning after Sally broke the news about Frank Streets. I rolled out of bed, grabbed my tie-dyed shirt and sweatpants off the floor, rubbed the sleep out of my eyes, and wandered downstairs to find my computer. It took a minute of hard staring at the screen before I mustered the courage to scour the web. I began with a reluctant click on the Blue Gray Ghost; I assumed he would already be all over the story, but he hadn't posted anything about Frank Streets's arrest. I was on the case before him.

This was my story.

I pulled my phone out of my sweatpants pocket and impulsively called Frank Streets. The phone rang a dozen times before the familiar sound of his voicemail message picked up. At least that was still working, I thought, and hung up without leaving a message. I dialed his cell phone, which quickly cut to a digitized voice informing me that the number was no longer in service.

Over the next few days, I called Frank Streets's office several times with no luck. I left a series of awkward messages, vaguely alluding to his arrest and wanting to "catch up," you know, like old pals might. I needed to see him before I left for Oaxaca. I needed something.

Just days before El and I were scheduled to leave, I called one last time, expecting nothing, resigned to writing off my relationship with Frank Streets for good.

"This is Frank Streets," his baritone voice bellowed, rattling my phone's tinny speaker.

"Frank! Hey, Frank, this is your old pal Steve West up in Morgantown," I said hopefully.

"What's going on, buddy." It was the real Frank Streets, and he sounded just like himself.

"I was just starting to worry about you," I laughed awkwardly. "I called your cell phone and it said it's disconnected."

"Yup, they have that," he said in a surly tone. "Confiscated it along with all of my computers and everything else when they raided the place." My mind flickered with footage of a SWAT team in navy blue fatigues with automatic weapons stomping all over his collection of animal skins.

"I was worried you were still in jail."

"Nope."

"Well, that's good to hear." I brainstormed how to bring up his arrest. "Are you still working?"

"Yep, still at it," he added. I could sense the trace of his spunky demeanor, maybe a bit wearier than usual.

"That's good, so, uh," I stuttered, unsure of how to broach the topic. "So, I read about what happened to you."

"I'm sure you did."

"Does this have anything to do with the sheriff?" I asked bluntly.

"Now, I'm not saying that." I could sense his eyes swirling with stories to tell. "Why don't you come on down and we'll talk, and we'll see what kind of story you can put together."

Scholars argue that the rise in popularity of hard-boiled detective fiction in the United States was a result of the shifting social landscape in the wake of the Great Depression. The era where masculinity was socially defined through the separation of spheres had necessarily changed. In the years between the world wars, women began to go to work to supplement family income in growing numbers, and a higher percentage of men were home than at any other time in American history. This rearrangement of gender roles at home following the women's movement for suffrage a generation before indicated a seismic shift in the social dimensions of men's lives, not to mention it unfolding amidst the political upheaval of two wars fought within a generation, wars in which more men died in combat than had in all of recorded history. Socially, politically, even physically, patriarchal privilege in America was necessarily shifting, and hard-boiled detective stories became a symbolic arena where men could encounter their crisis of masculinity in terms familiar to the Self-Made Man in crisis: a cutthroat world where threats came from all sides and men struggled to achieve success through any means necessary.

These books offered men the fantasy of self-preservation through physical dominance, misogynistic violence, and the stiff upper lip that they craved. Hammett's *The Maltese Falcon* is the pinnacle of hard-boiled fiction, and Sam Spade is the cover boy of the brand of private investigators American men fantasized about. Solitary and gruff with street smarts for days, Sam Spade is a gritty and ruthless man's man always prepared for a jawing or a gunfight with a flask in his jacket and a dame on his arm. Fearless, confident, and driven, Sam Spade is the new version of the Self-Made Man born in the current of the crisis of masculinity, lean and mean and equipped to handle the volatile landscape of gender relationships in the twentieth century, a champion for how white, American men could maintain their authority in an era that threatened them.

Take for example how *The Maltese Falcon* begins. Within the first chapter, a reader meets Sam Spade in his office, handsome and strong with a face like a "blonde Satan" as he barks orders at his secretary, licks his chops and smiles at the woman who walks into his office looking for help finding a lost statuette of a black bird. Then, after investigating the site where his partner was murdered shadowing a known criminal for his client, Sam Spade returns to his office to change the shingle on the street to remove his partner's name without a single tear in his eye; when his partner's widow—who Sam Spade is having an affair with—collapses into his arms, he shoos her away with a growl, avoiding her for the remainder of the novel. Sam Spade shows no wince of fear in the face of the police questioning him about his connection to the murder, nor does he quiver when a foreigner in search of the same missing statuette saunters into his office and points a pistol at his chest, which Sam Spade takes away with brutal ease.

For an average man, this much upheaval and intrigue in a year would break them, but for Sam Spade, he remains in control, his jaw and scowl set as he remains in power over the countless people that vie for control over him. He simply pours himself drink after drink, his dangerous yellow-gray eyes and wolfish smile pointing out to women and non-white people—and all other white men, too—that he will come out on top in the end by any means necessary.

"I can't have my guns," Frank Streets lamented, his gaze moving from me to the empty pool table as I closed the sliding door and walked into his den. There were no firearms anywhere in sight, punctuated by the three cabinets along the back wall devoid of weapons. To my relief, the collection of hunting plunder that pawed, crouched, and pounced on every surface was intact and as resplendent as ever.

"When you have a felony charge against you, guns are one of those things you can't have." Frank Streets looked forlornly around his den. "Standard procedure for everyone. You can't leave the state, can't go to an establishment that serves alcoholic beverages, and can't have guns." He shook his head ruefully, and I could see how this was a crucial departure for him, a part of his identity that had been stripped away for the first time in his life.

We made small talk in his den, and he started in about the extra time he had on his hands since he'd been kicked off all his criminal cases, thanks to the indictment. At worst, the charges levied against him carried a six-month sentence, and Frank Streets seemed unruffled by the threat of time in the clink. The real issue was if he were found guilty, he'd lose his private investigator's license. As he surveyed his disarmed den, I could see the glint of fear in his eyes when he mentioned that—as if losing his ability to be a PI—losing that part of his identity—was a fate he couldn't imagine.

We walked into his office and took our familiar seats facing each other across his heavy oak desk.

"So, the arrest," I prompted. Frank Streets pursed his mouth in response and stared at me. Something had changed between us. I was a writer with a recorder now—I was the investigator. I had a power over him that I hadn't had before. I held my breath, the weight of that implication making my body larger in his presence, the sweat on my brow more visible than I was comfortable with.

I waited in silence, holding eye contact with him like a teacher playing chicken with a student after asking a difficult question.

"It was related to the case in Shinnston," he began. "Where Junkins was alleged to be taking drugs out of the evidence room. To give to this boy CJ Wilson to sell. That case was about to go to trial." His staccato cadence was unlike anything I'd heard from Frank Streets before. It made me nervous that he was so measured when in the past he had always been so open.

"On Friday, May 17, I'm raided," he continued. "I'm arrested. Eleven officers show up. Guns drawn. I was getting ready to go out for dinner. They handcuffed me, set me out on the swing under the deck in the driveway. There were two or three officers out there with AR-15s, all in bulletproof vests. Like they were raiding a big drug dealer." He allowed a slight chuckle to hiss free from his tense form.

"So, I'm confused," I said, knitting my brow and crossing my legs. "What did you do?" I cringed. "I mean, what are they saying you did?" I leaned forward and knotted my hands across my knee; I stared as long as I could at Frank Streets, my eyes hot and watery. He stared hard back at me.

Of course, I was being coy. When I scoured the local news, I found that Frank Streets was indicted on two felony charges: conspiracy to commit threats in official and political matters and making threats in official and political matters. He was also indicted on three misdemeanor charges: conspiracy to commit witness intimidation, obstruction of a law enforcement officer, and conspiracy to commit obstruction of a law enforcement officer.

Frank Streets's buddy Paul Harris was also indicted that day on one count of felony conspiracy to commit threats in official and political matters and on the same three misdemeanor counts.

Harrison County Prosecutor Joe Shaffer was quoted in the *Exponent Telegram* as saying that the charges against both Harris and Streets arose "out of the alleged interference with a witness" in the case against former Shinnston policeman Kevin B. Junkins, Jr.: the case that Frank Streets was investigating when he heard the story that multiple cops besides Junkins were stealing drugs and trading them for sexual favors—the discovery that made Frank Streets a marked man who had to watch what he said over the phone in Shinnston on the day we lost the adulterer.

I knew all of this, but I wanted to hear Frank Streets's story.

"When CJ met with me earlier that week, he was wearing a video and a wire." Frank Streets's eyes were fixed on mine. "They got me on two felonies—obstructing a law enforcement officer and intimidating witnesses. On the video CJ recorded," he gestured with his chin at a pile of CDs next to his computer monitor, "I've got a copy of it right there from the prosecutor's office—you can see I pick him up and we're talking. I asked him what he's gonna do, and he said he's going to the carnival in Buchannon. I asked him what he wanted to go there for, you can hear it right on the audio," Frank Streets said defensively. "He's wanting to take his kids to a carnival, the strawberry festival in Buchannon. So, I'm sitting there drawing him a map to get to the carnival, and he makes a comment, don't give up your day job 'cause you're an awful map drawer,'" Frank Streets laughed gruffly, then looked at me expectantly.

I chuckled dutifully but wasn't sure why he would be drawing a map at all for CJ. Why did he care if CJ found the carnival or not? It seemed strange to be doing that with a key witness for a trial that was just days away. It seemed like Frank Streets would know that could be used against him.

"Then I get out, I walk around the car and talk to CJ's wife for a second. She says she feels like blowing her head off." It was an odd detail to highlight. Frank Streets had told me that CJ's wife was still addicted to heroin, and I wondered if her comment was related to that, or, if she was feeling stress for some unspoken reason, like having to skip town days before a trial where she and her husband were key witnesses.

"After I talked with her," Frank Streets continued, "I get back in the truck and I said, 'if you're going now, you can follow me up there and I'll show you what exit to take, then you can do your own thing.'" Frank Streets was a helpful guy, but I had to admit his level of good Samaritanism with two heroin addicts just days before a case he was working went to trial—a case where they were key witnesses for the prosecution—was odd to say the least.

Frank Streets plucked a CD off a stack on his desk and inserted it in his computer tower. Shaky footage of a skinny, tattooed kid with an oversized T-shirt and baggy jeans appeared on the screen. This was CJ: his voice was high-pitched, and he spoke with a thick Appalachian drawl. The tinny audio was distorted by the whines of a young child somewhere in the background. CJ spoke directly to the screen, flashing $300 in twenties to the officer working the camera.

"Who gave this to you," the officer asked from off screen, and CJ enunciated soberly, "Frank Streets," as if he were already on the stand giving testimony. Then, CJ began to fidget, looking away from the camera and scratching his neck aggressively. He began muttering something else under his breath when the officer cut him off, ordering him to count the money for the camera, which he did slowly. "Three hundred dollars right there. Good job," the officer said, and the video ended. It wasn't clear what the officer was congratulating CJ for doing.

"But there's no money being exchanged, nothing about money on the video CJ recorded in my truck!" Frank Streets blurted, his jaw unhinged, his eyes desperate as they met mine.

He reached over to his computer keyboard and stopped the video, stretching to the side, loosening his neck. I remained still.

"But the thing about it is," he said, recomposing his grimace into a hard scowl and leaning toward me, "when they raided my place, they took eleven USB drives, and all of my disks with all of my statements." He paused dramatically, my brain scrambling to keep afloat in the abrupt shifts that were a signature of his brand of storytelling. "Statements for all of my cases," he repeated slowly. Not just the Junkins case." Frank Streets lurched forward and shouted, his giant fist crashing down like a gavel on his desk. "You see they had to get a felony on me, so they could come arrest me. It doesn't take a genius to see the raid was a fishing expedition. It doesn't take a genius to see that they wanted the information from my investigation of the sheriff." He leaned back, his upper lip curled with rage. "There are thirty-six girls with statements against the sheriff in that case."

"Thirty-six girls with allegations against the sheriff?" I sat stunned. This was so many more young women with accusations than even Blue Gray Ghost had been insinuating on his blog.

"Yes. I wasn't withholding any of them. I'd given all of them to Fast Freddie and the FBI." Frank Streets leaned toward me, weaving his fingers together on his desk like a cat's cradle. "When they went and arrested Paul Harris, they didn't take any of his files," he snarled. "None."

The room shrunk as he whispered angrily and my body returned to normal size. "The prosecution has every sworn statement I have against the sheriff on my recorder. Every statement from every single girl." He stood up to lean even closer to me, his teeth bared. "And they still have that recorder."

"Since I was arrested, I've received three phone calls from girls I took sworn statements from in that investigation wanting to know why I released their information. I had to tell them I didn't release nothin'. I had to tell them that Harrison County authorities have their statements," he said angrily. "So that means somebody has contacted these girls and said, 'You've talked to Frank Streets. I've got your telephone number, your street address, and I have what you said to him.'" He looked away in disgust. "I promised those girls I would keep them anonymous."

"The day after I'm arrested, on the sheriff's Facebook, a Harrison County deputy says how good it was working in Barbour County, bragging about what he did out here. So I printed it. Hawkins deleted it, but it's too late, because I did print it."

"They were bragging about arresting you?"

"They didn't mention my name, but," he said, and went and grabbed the printout. He walked back to the desk, reading aloud from the Facebook post:

"'Got to work with one of your deputies Friday. I think one of them has a brother that works for me.' Now here's what Hawkins replies, 'I know it's not good to take joy in others sorrow. We are taught to pray even for our enemies but it's hard when all the people that cause me and my family so much grief seem to be falling off one by one.' This came from Sheriff Hawkins's Facebook." Frank Streets eyed me as he sat down in his chair, gauging my reaction. "The deputy that led the raid on my house and served me the indictment, that's the one responding to Hawkins right there." He pointed at the thumbnail of his Facebook profile pic.

He handed me the copy of the Facebook post, and I read

it quietly. "It doesn't say your name directly, but it sure does seem related," I conceded.

"See the date?" he said, his meaty finger pointing at the page. "That's the next day, after I was arrested." He tapped the date several times, the paper rattling in my hand.

"So, they went and made straw-man felonies so they could get the information you were finding out about the sheriff— that's what they really wanted," I puzzled aloud, thinking it sounded like a setup straight out of a hard-boiled novel.

But as I listened to Frank Streets rationalize why the charges against him were a conspiracy by the authorities to get their hands on his case files, I couldn't help but notice that he didn't deny that he asked CJ to lie. I couldn't help but observe that he was talking his way around what really happened in that video footage, whether consciously or not.

He was prioritizing a conspiracy theory for why he was ar-rested, putting the viability of the indictment in the crosshairs rather than the truth of the allegations against him.

"That day in your truck with CJ," I began hesitantly as Frank Streets escorted me out of his office. "I mean, why were you meeting him? And where did that money even come from?" I asked with a chuckle, trying to hide the importance of this information I was seeking beneath the naive writer shtick that Frank Streets was familiar with. We had spent the morn-ing theorizing conspiracies for why he was arrested, but I still wondered about the actual charges against him.

"Here is the truth about something," Frank Streets said, stopping in front of the sliding glass doors in his den. He looked wistfully at the landscape across Valley View Road, to the creek and woods beyond. "The day I met with CJ and he was wired, I had three hundred dollars in my notebook in the console. I don't know when it came up missing." I understood how something might get misplaced in his truck; I had seen the piles of gear in Frank Streets's center console, and how binoculars, various recording devices, CB radios, tins of snuff, granola bars, notebooks, and pee bottles all pile upon each other haphazardly. But I'd never seen envelopes with wads of money lying around.

"It had to be done when I stepped out to talk to his wife. He was still sitting in the car, and my notebook was sitting right between us. And he'd seen the envelope," Frank Streets said. "Because I flipped it up like this to draw the map," and he mimed opening his notebook. I wasn't sure how CJ would just assume the envelope had money in it. And why Frank Streets would vividly remember flashing an envelope full of money at CJ. This was the most tenuous part of the story so far. All I could conclude for certain: Frank Streets had money when he met CJ. Then, after that meeting, CJ had money.

"But what's the logic? Why would you be paying him?" I asked, and scowled, peeking to gauge his reaction.

"That morning, CJ calls me and says, 'I'm out of money.' I sent my text back and said, 'I'm sorry, what can I do about it?' he sent me a text saying, 'Leaving here, just like to meet with you for a brief minute.' I write back, 'Okay, but I will not give you any money, I have never paid a witness and I never will.'"

"You texted all that back?" I gulped at how deliberate and scripted it seemed—and how irresponsible it would have been to then leave him alone with money in his truck. I instinctually looked down at my feet and kept my gaze there.

But here's the thing I never told anybody." Frank Streets paused to measure his words. I held my breath. "I knew CJ was in hiding. But I'm not under no obligation—none—to pick up the phone and call Prosecuting Attorney Joe Shaffer to tell him that. If he calls me, I can't lie to them, but I don't have to tell them anything. They never once contacted me. Nor did anyone from the sheriff's office contact me. But, yeah, I did know he was in hiding."

I drove automatically on the highway back to Morgantown, my form pulled down by the same gravity as always, but I felt finally aware of the influence it always holds over me. My face was clay as I stared through the montage of mountains upon mountains and exit ramp strip malls that flickered by in fast-forward. My heart beat into my throat: the one and only Franklin D. Streets, Jr. was caught in the crosshairs of a corrupt justice system with multiple officials from neighboring counties conspiring to take him down.

Or he was lying. About all of it.

"The phrase itself 'innocent until proven guilty' is actually derived from presumption of innocence that is the most basic in our system of justice," Blue Gray Ghost writes. "This basic right comes to us like so many other things, from English jurisprudence and has been part of the system for so long that it is considered common law." But not everyone follows that law. More often than not when someone is publicly accused of a crime we presume they are guilty until it is proven otherwise.

"Take for example the recent allegations made against the Barbour County Sheriff, John Hawkins," Blue Gray Ghost explains. "There are many of us that have already formed an opinion; some of us have presumed guilt, while others have presumed innocence and some have remained neutral. So the question remains, why are we already forming defined perceptions with just an allegation?"

"Why would you or Paul Harris or anybody want CJ to miss the trial? I just don't understand," I said to no one as I stared at the space between the yellow lines unfurling on the highway. "Why would you want to screw over the prosecution's case? And why the hell would they care about your investigation of the sheriff from a neighboring county?" It didn't add up. "Why would you put yourself on the line for this case, Frank? Of all the cases you've worked. Why this one? Why did you do it?" I growled at the road ahead. Frank Streets's eyes simmered in the courtroom of my imagination, his teeth bared as he dramatically shouted, You can't handle the truth!

"Is anyone truly innocent until proven guilty," Blue Gray Ghost concludes, "or is everyone truly guilty until innocence can be proven?"

❉

I was a miserable piece of shit in Oaxaca. I felt stuck in a crowded foreign country where I couldn't speak the language, living day and night as the primary caregiver of an energetic, curious, exhausted nine-month-old who required constant feeding, diaper changes, and naps. But the parenting was the best part. The Spanish-style hacienda we rented had flimsy cabana-style doors that posed the only barrier between our quarters and the owner's on the other side of the small court-yard, an expatriate American named Shari who had just had facial reconstructive surgery and hadn't left since we arrived because of the monstrous appearance of her face as it healed.

In other words, El and I were trapped inside our side of the hacienda as Shari continued living like always, i.e., talking on the phone with her other expat friends about her face and all the drama among the expat diva community in Oaxaca she was missing out on.

We had picked this place over a hotel because it was in the cultural district of Oaxaca, within walking distance of the city's main square and dozens of restaurants, coffee shops, and art galleries. We were under the impression that our hacienda had a private open-air courtyard, and while K was off following candidates' campaigns, sometimes for several days at a time, El and I would bask in the sun, eating mangos in perpetual slow motion and watching chicatana ants forage on the tile floor, giggling like we were on party drugs, him at their comic size, and me at the idea of the salsa dip they would be cooked into. The courtyard was open-air and lush with banana trees and ficus and a water feature just like we'd seen in the pictures, but it was a postage stamp, and it was far from private.

El was uncomfortable and fussy; he missed his mama, and his routines, like mine, had been toppled. I spent the majority of my days in Oaxaca huddling in the windowless interior of our half of the hacienda problem-solving how to soothe El to sleep so I could lie down and rub my temples. Not to mention my guts were squirming with cramps that sent me sprinting to the toilet in a cold sweat every thirty minutes, and those few moments pissing from my ass were sacred; I closed my eyes and took Buddha breaths while I shat until El started to fuss in the other room, pleased in a sinister way that the open air windows revealed all the twists and turns of my bathroom use to Shari as she gabbed on her phone about her bloodshot eyes and bruised lips.

When K and I had planned that I would come to Oaxaca, there was no reason I shouldn't. Frank Streets hadn't been arrested, and I had all but given up on my aspirations to write a book about him.

But I agreed to travel to Oaxaca because I was sold on the romance of traveling to Oaxaca. I fancied I would be the artist abroad, finding inspiration in the simple, exotic, peculiar nature of life there, writing all my big important thoughts about it. It would be the month-long writer's residency I had a habit of getting rejected from, their lovely letters notifying of my failure plastered to my canvas. I had even asked writer friends what books I should take to read that would inspire me to write in some creative rage, my book unfurling in single, perfect scroll as I typed in a Kerouacian fever dream for days without sleep, lighting cigarettes off one another and drinking mescal and howling at the Mexican moon, I've finally done it! I am a writer! But I had overlooked how many diapers would need to be changed and how many bottles of formula would need to be made, and how far I would feel from the suave writer with a moleskin notebook I wanted to be when I ventured into the city in my gringo cargo shorts and boat shoes with an oversized stroller and an angry baby.

"Have you read Geoff Dyer's *Out of Sheer Rage*?" my friend Torrey asked innocently when she offered some ideas for what books I should take with me to Oaxaca. "You really should. It's a book about his failure to write a book."

"That hurts," I joked as I scribbled the title down. It was the only book I ended up taking with me.

"It's about D. H. Lawrence. I think Dyer even went to Oaxaca in it, because Lawrence would go there."

Lawrence did go to "Beastly Oaxaca," and so did Dyer, so that was an ironic overlap, but not as ironic as I felt it was that I was reading Dyer's well-written and undoubtedly published book about not writing a book about D. H. Lawrence, unless I was hallucinating from my epic case of traveler's diarrhea. I admit I found some pleasure in the fact that Dyer went to Oaxaca and didn't do a single thing related to his goal to write about Lawrence; he failed miserably as a writer there, and he didn't even have a nine-month-old to blame it on.

A few hours after I put El to bed each night, I might have mustered some energy to write or check on Blue Gray Ghost, see how far ahead of me he was getting on uncovering the truth beneath the corruption in West Virginia, but K would sneak in through the humid evening air and we would eat and drink and talk together. It was nice, but it wasn't romantic. She was exhausted from her work, and I spent time complaining about how hard my days were, lamenting over how unhappy I was in Oaxaca and instead of being home chasing down the truth in The Case of Frank Streets. K would quietly listen, holding back the frustrations she felt over the constant trials she faced as a smart, attractive American woman with compromised eyesight on the campaign trail in the phallocentric world of Mexican politics. She would hold all of that in and quietly plan for the next day of work, stoically filing away the emotional stress that I dumped on her because I was frustrated that my life required me to be exclusively a parent and a husband when my desire was to write about Frank Streets.

Why did Frank Streets get out of his truck and leave a heroin addict sitting alone with his $300? Unless he left the money there for him. But why would Frank Streets want CJ to skip the trial? What made the Junkins case so important that Frank Streets would put his reputation on the line for it? But I couldn't get to the bottom of those questions. The responsibilities I owed to El and K had become an obstacle.

It was early afternoon and still humid and hot about half-way through my time in Oaxaca when I felt an urgent need to do something related to my identity, not just be a parent hiding from Shari's plastic surgery. Despite the size of our stroller, I decided it was time to take El to the Museo de los Pintores Oaxaqueños in the Zocalo, Oaxaca's city center. The Zocalo was about a thirty-minute walk from our hacienda, but I didn't care; I had to feel like a person I recognized, and an art museum was just the elixir for what I craved.

Along the way, El and I walked through a large market. The markets in central Oaxaca are lined with artists selling their work, from enormous abstract sculptures to paintings, etchings, and prints. Oaxaca is known for its alebrijes, small wood carvings of animals and insects that are delicately painted with shockingly bright colors. The more intricate alebrijes are pricey, but coarsely carved and painted versions are cheap and easy to find in the markets. I figured I could muster enough Spanish to buy one for El to chew on in the museum to help with his teething.

After I scoured the tables of jade-colored jewelry, skulls carved from obsidian, and handmade paper dolls, I found an alebrije that fit perfectly in El's fist: a blocky orange fish I named Nemo after the movie we had watched together on my laptop several times already since we'd been in Oaxaca. As I was paying for it, I noticed an artist's display with strikingly colored prints. The works were vibrant, graphic compositions in indigo, burnt orange, and forest green. The artist was a lithe and tan man with long silver hair, who wore a pair of faded blue jeans like someone not from Oaxaca. I stopped to look at his work, which I rarely do, because I get uncomfortable when artists watch me look at their work, waiting for a reaction, like Dani from the Blue Moose and the forgettable blobby landscape paintings she showed me on her phone. I avoid eye contact and smile humbly, like I would whenever I ordered coffee from her at the Blue Moose after that day; but in Oaxaca I didn't care. I was drawn to this artist. He looked like I wanted to look; a natural and cool and confident man as he leaned with his arms crossed, the only one not sweating in my field of vision, a soul more than a person with an air of commitment to an ideal that he actually pulled off.

"Hola," he said gently.

"Hola, hello," I replied stiffly, appreciative in a way that he spoke Spanish to me in spite of my perfect rendition of gringo-dad-with-lily-white-baby.

"I am from Oaxaca," he continued in English, "but I studied art at the royal academy at the University of London. I make my own ink from the landscape. The orange ink is from the soil of Monte Alban." Monte Alban is a site of Zapotec ruins situated atop a mountain outside of the city, one of the few places K, El, and I were able to visit together.

"They're beautiful," I remarked sincerely.

"It's an interpretation of a Zapotec creation myth." He nodded to an orange etching of what looked like a man with an avian head dancing on a mountain, his head pointed to the sky.

"Go ahead, touch it."

"No. I can't," I muttered and laughed awkwardly.

"Artists rarely tell patrons to touch their work," he smiled comfortably. He knew I wasn't going to buy one of his etchings, but he earnestly wanted me to touch his art, and that gesture felt important to me, and I could see it was important to him. I looked at his eyes as I ran my fingers over the ridges of ink pressed into the print, feeling the gravelly texture of the soil from the ruins of Monte Alban.

When we arrived at the museum, I was so sweaty and El was puffy and red and starting to complain. I wasn't allowed to take the stroller through the museum. I had to carry El, and he started to fuss immediately as his cheek kept sticking to my forearm and my sweat kept dripping down the bridge of my nose and onto him. But I didn't give a fuck. I was determined to look at every goddamn room and work of art.

The works were mostly ink and watercolor and pretty

enough, but they become wallpaper in a few minutes. None of them were as lovely as the market artist's etchings. I thought about the prestige museums carry, how they validate the quality of a work of art—and an artist by extension—yet how bloodless they are. The art is still and quiet and quarantined by velvet ropes, and people lean in toward it, holding their breath with their arms behind their backs, obligated to admire it. It wasn't for me, with my sweat and body odor, my pulse vibrating under the weight of the fidgety baby in my arms. My thoughts drifted to the artist in the market, how his work was the kind you can touch.

As El got heavier and heavier in my arms, I resigned to reading the names and numbers on placards more than examining the works themselves. I read n. 1981, n. 1984, n. 1990, assuming they represented the year the work was made. But each work had two dates: 2008, 2010, 2012, and it hit me: n. stands for nacido, meaning the artist's birth year. With El mere minutes from breaking down into tears and in need of a nap and cooler temperatures (I can read his moods before they arrive), I stormed through the museum to prove that I could do it all, noting every single artist was younger than me and how I hadn't accomplished anything even close to their success yet, how I was tired of feeling like a fraud, tired of feeling like a failure, and tired of being afraid to confront the truth that who I really was required letting go of the man I desired to be.

It's not a stretch to see how *The Maltese Falcon* reveals the way men were likely to feel uneasy about their masculinity in twentieth-century America. Throughout the novel, there's an unspoken struggle to figure out who is the manly man, and this plays out in the conflicts among the characters. It is in Sam Spade's abusive and violent interactions with the women in the novel, actions that critics say are driven by his desire to maintain control over them as a way to enforce a social order, that his sense of manhood is preserved. It is through this that Sam Spade becomes the epitome of the fearful white American man faced with a crisis of his masculinity.

Sam Spade's relationship with his secretary, Effie Perine, seems the least problematic, or at least the most conventional; their interactions smack of conventional male–female work relationships where men are in charge and responsible for the "real" work while women are there to listen and serve the men and literally keep the lights on. In this way, his relationship with Perine is terra firma for a male reader in that it reinforces traditional gendered power dynamics. Sam Spade exploits Perine's diligence and loyalty, taking for granted that she will dote upon his whims and sacrifice herself for him at a moment's notice. Perine is the most stable character in the novel, and Sam Spade takes full advantage of the stability her subservience to a conventional gender hierarchy affords.

Sam Spade's relationship with Iva Archer also plays out according to what men would expect from the women in their lives. Archer is the telltale spurned lover, hysterical and desperate over her unrequited love for Sam Spade. Her only desire is for Sam Spade to acknowledge her emotionally—and to own up to his promise to marry her. But it seems his promise was so much pillow talk; Archer's feelings are the collateral damage of Sam Spade's sexual conquest of her. He coldly shuns her, avoids her calls, and chastises her. Nothing in his demeanor or actions shows care, let alone respect, for her. He avoids her at all costs—often employing Perine to throw Archer off his trail—so he can deal with the book's most compelling female character, Brigid O'Shaughnessy.

Sam Spade's relationship with O'Shaughnessy is the most contentious among any of the characters in that he has the least control over her. Their relationship is confrontational and competitive, their interactions marked by sexual tension, deception, and outright physical abuse. They are in direct competition for the Maltese falcon—the prize with the promise of immeasurable fortune that both O'Shaughnessy and Sam

Spade want to cash in on. In their attempts to gain the statuette they relentlessly manipulate each other, playing as many sides as they can to get the falcon and assume the power it represents. Sam Spade ultimately wins the battle, but not without demolishing all the women in his path, including physically forcing O'Shaughnessy to undress in front of him to prove she didn't steal his money, eventually turning her in to the police for her partner's murder. But even that move is not honorable; Sam Spade does it to protect his own neck from the police detectives out to pin several murders on him.

Sam Spade's practice of insightful analysis and deductive reasoning allow him to seize control in every conflict he encounters. He uses his intellectual ability to subdue the women he views as adversaries to his desire, thus keeping them in line with a gender order that preserves his masculinity.

K returned to our hacienda that evening after a full day of research with a six-pack of Bohemia beer and some quesadillas made with queso Oaxaqueño she picked up at a market. El and I were both exhausted when we finally made it back from our trip to the museum, and he melted into such a blubbering mess from heat exhaustion and hunger that it took me an hour to soothe him to sleep.

K was leaving for a remote part of Mexico the next morning and would be gone for two nights before returning on the third day. She was dreading the trip, the longest she was planning to be apart from us during our time in Oaxaca. We ate and drank together on the day bed in our small living area trying to enjoy the few minutes we had with each other. I enjoyed the conversation in English, having spent most days silent if I wasn't describing the size of the ants, the color of the sewer grates, or intense heat and rain to El.

She told me about her research trip to Zimatlan that day, the thousands of people she watched line up for handouts of food and water and medicine from political candidates, the woman whose sweat dripped off her nose and into a large barrel of punch as she plunged her arm down to her elbow to scoop cup after cup for the people lined up for it. K was witnessing first-hand how patronage matters more to voters in developing areas than policy—the central theory of her book validated every single day through boots-on-the-ground research, a method that no one had ever used before to measure this theory. She felt proud about how important it was going to make her work.

I didn't share with her my experience with the artist that let me touch his art, instead telling her about the two young Mexican women I met in the market, how they had babies around the same age as El, how we smiled at each other knowingly but couldn't talk about our responsibilities even though I wanted to, the two toddlers that then ran up to El and started touching him, and how it was cute until they tried to take his pacifier, how El said "DaDa" so I figured I should take him to a museum since he had clearly been reading twentieth-century art history, and the stunning success of getting him to eat a piece of actual banana. She told me how proud I should feel, how important my work as a parent was.

"What do I have to be proud of," I sneered. "My fucking kid ate a banana!"

"He said your name." Her lip quivered. "I want him to say my name. It just makes me feel like I'm missing everything because of this stupid book."

I placed my beer down on the table deliberately. "Seriously? You're serious right now?" My heart vibrated along its most fragile fault line.

"Yes! I'm serious," she glared. "I want to feed him bananas, to have him say my name. Yes, I am jealous! What does it matter what I'm doing out here—so what if I write a book. This is what matters, this," she said, wildly lassoing our living space with her arm.

"What, this? Shari's shitty hacienda that we hide in all day?"

She laughed spitefully. "You hide in all day. You are the one hiding, Steve. All you've done is complain this entire time, and I can tell you don't want to be here with me." Tears welled up in her eyes. "Or with your son. What do you want? What will make you happy?"

"You have a career with promise! I'm a fucking wannabe. At the museum today, all the art was by artists younger than me. What have I done? You're doing something important, you're writing a book. I want to do something important, too."

"You are," she said, still glaring at me.

"I'm only here for you—we're only here for you," I snarled and pointed toward El's room, "because you were selfish and couldn't be apart from us for a month. I mean I get it. I do. I felt bad for you. He's your baby, and you have your book to write, but I'm paying for it being stuck here doing nothing. I hate being a fucking sucker for emotional decisions, always taking care of everyone else and not myself."

"You're a sucker?" K raised her voice. "You?" Her eyes prickled with electricity. "I'm the sucker. I'm the sucker to think you could actually come here and not put yourself first for once, that you could take care of me and your son and see how important that is. And who knows? Actually enjoy yourself and live for what you have instead of what you don't. I'm the sucker." She looked away. "I just don't know what will make you happy," she whispered and shook her head. She looked at me with pity, and I have never felt like more of a failure.

While Sam Spade is too flawed to be one of Auden's professional detectives, his shrewd intellect and keen gift of insight rivals the best of the sleuths in houndstooth jackets. But Sam Spade is a hard-boiled detective, after all—he is not an agent of ethics, and the only state of grace he seeks to return to is one where his position of masculine dominance is secured. His desire to preserve his power is at the heart of the external conflict of *The Maltese Falcon*; it is what drives his desire to solve the riddle of the statuette and get his hands on it before anyone else. But his anxiety over threats to the gender order drives him, too, to the point where he ruthlessly sacrifices opportunities for love and companionship with the women he subjugates at every turn. He resorts to hurting the women in his life to protect the pursuit of his desires, and when that pursuit is threatened—and by extension, when his masculinity is threatened—he lashes out to preserve the control over his identity that he desperately clings to.

Sam Spade can only be viewed as an exemplar of male fantasy in an age where the gender order is in crisis. There is no doubt that he is a threatened, fearful man. He has no money; he has no wife or children; he trusts no one and allows no one to trust him. He is a stick figure so consumed by his fear of losing control over the man he believes himself to be—the man he demands others allow him to be—that he becomes a toxic expression of delusional Self-Made Manhood in crisis.

"It's plastic-coated wire. You can put it around the neck and hold it down, take the trap off and release it. Like dog catchers." Frank Streets walked to the corner of his den, past several piles of large animal traps with comically jagged teeth. He picked up the long steel rod with a noose attached to the end and pointed it at me. "I caught the neighbor's cat," he said, looking contemplatively at the noose. I looked at the menacing jaws of the trap, hoping not to see blood. "Let it go the first time. A couple weeks later I caught it again and let it go again. Then it came up missing," he added dryly. I grinned and squelched out a nervous laugh, not sure if the irony was intentional. He returned the noose to the wall, where there were a dozen wooden racks with animal hides draped on them. There were half a dozen large white buckets by the sliding glass door, and the entire floor stretching between the pool table and his office was covered two-feet deep with sphagnum moss.

"Right up to the day she died she swore up and down I killed that cat," Frank Streets said through his trademark grin.

"You'd be my number-one suspect, too."

He nodded and frowned. "But see the thing is right now, deer season is right around the corner, and I still don't have my guns." Frank Streets looked just as formidable as always, but his hair was unslicked, longer on the temples than I'd seen before. His full beard and a buffalo plaid flannel complemented his renewed commitment to trapping; it was mid-October, the eve of hunting season and Frank Streets's favorite time of year, but the first of his life when he'd been accused of multiple felonies.

"They're hitting you where it hurts," I said.

"Yeah, I've never not been able to carry my gun," he shook his head in disbelief, and I pictured Frank Streets as a toddler with a rifle in his crib. "I'm gonna take this whole winter off, and just trap. I always trap along the crick up the road here. It's got a lot of muskrat and beaver. I always use the muskrat carcass."

"For what?" I asked, unsure what use a carcass could ever have.

"I make my own lure. When I catch bobcats, mink, once I skin them, I cut the glands. Got an old blender down in my building, and I grind the stuff up."

"You got a serious operation here," I said trying to unscrew my face and stomach at the thought of that blender.

"You couldn't get in here yesterday, the whole floor was covered with tarps and about five dozen traps. I'd had to boil them out in the driveway, that's what that stain was." I hadn't noticed the stain but planned to avoid stepping in it on the way back to my car.

"I'd love one of your hides," I said sincerely.

"What do you want?" Frank Streets stared at me with business eyes.

"Something cool," I laughed dumbly. "What's your

favorite?"

"Probably fox. I've caught upwards of two hundred of those before." I thought he was playing me, but he didn't blink.

I took a deep breath, my smile vanishing into a frown. I knew Frank Streets would be content to stand in his den and talk about trapping for hours. Hell, he'd probably even demo the blender for me if I asked, but it wasn't why I'd driven to Valley View Road. I'd come down for the first time since returning from Oaxaca because Sherman Lambert, Frank Streets's defense attorney, had recused himself from representing Frank Streets and the charges against him. The news reported that the trial, originally scheduled for the end of October, was delayed until Frank Streets found new counsel.

I was out to find why Frank Streets's lawyer had requested to be recused from the trial, but I really wanted to dig deeper into Frank Streets's conspiracy theory. I could see why the sheriff would have it out for Frank Streets because of his investigation into the allegations against him. Especially if there were thirty-six girls with something to say about it. But if Frank Streets had been framed, the sheriff didn't pull it off: he couldn't even have brought charges against him if he wanted to. Frank Streets's felony charges were related to the Junkins case—a case in neighboring Harrison county. It seemed too much like a crime novel for the prosecuting attorney from a neighboring county to be framing Frank Streets as a favor to a sheriff of another county—especially when that sheriff was under investigation by the FBI. Why would Prosecuting Attorney Joe Shaffer want the information Frank Streets had gathered on the sheriff? And beyond that, why would he want to bring Frank Streets to his knees? Any validity to the conspiracy balanced precariously on that answer.

I also hoped Frank Streets might know when his trial would take place. I had decided I would be at the trial as a character witness or just as a concerned party, holding his wife's hand in the balcony, fanning her with a newspaper, embracing her as she shuddered with tears as the verdict came down with an uproar only muted when the curtains closed on The Trial of Frank Streets. I had made it my Maltese falcon; I secretly hoped for it, needed it, and felt ashamed that I wanted Frank Streets to be found guilty because it would be the best conclusion to any book I might write about him.

"So, the last time we chatted," I began vaguely, "last time I was down here was right after your indictment." I looked at him.

"Really," he replied cautiously, looking around at his den.

"I went to Mexico with my family right after that, believe it or not," I said, hoping to lure him into a casual conversation to warm things up, but he didn't take the bait. "Can you believe it's been that long?" I chattered.

"Huh."

"I've been wondering about a couple things," I croaked and rubbed my forehead. "I can see why the sheriff would want to take you down, but why the prosecuting attorney from Harrison County? Why Joe Shaffer? What skin does he have in the game?"

Frank Streets wearily led me to his office. He grabbed a paper from the printer and handed it to me. It was a news article from the *Exponent Telegram*. In addition to his meticulous process of duplicating recordings and case files, Frank Streets obsessively archives hard copies of news coverage of every case he works on. In some cases, he has multiple copies kept in separate locations for added security.

The headline on the paper he handed me mentioned a suicide in Clarksburg. I looked at the date: five months before his indictment.

"This is a case I was investigating for my former counsel, Sherman Lambert." We sat in awkward silence. Frank Streets snatched the paper out of my hand and snapped it open. "'Kelly'—that's the mother of the suicide—'her attorney Sherman Lambert says he wants a full investigation by authorities,'" he read aloud. "'He's also hired a private investigator from Barbour County, Frank Streets, on behalf of the family.'"

On the morning of January 7, Michael Joseph Kelly was found dead in his mother's house in Clarksburg. He was on house arrest at the time as part of his bond release on charges of grand larceny, wanton endangerment, and burglary. His mother returned home at 8 a.m. to find her son hanging from an electrical cord in the middle of the room.

Questions swirled around Kelly's death. The night of his alleged suicide, he had been visiting relatives in the Clarksburg area, and police had video showing Kelly at a GoMart around 2 a.m. buying alcohol. Muddying the events leading to his death even further, Kelly's GPS monitoring bracelet reportedly went dead after midnight. When that occurs, the home confinement office is supposed to be immediately notified electronically that the GPS is offline. That never happened.

Even more peculiar, the Clarksburg Police had been called to the Kelly residence on a loud music complaint and had seen Kelly still alive around 4:30 a.m.

"They ruled it suicide," Frank Streets said. "This is the case I was investigating that the prosecuting attorney, Joe Shaffer, was ticked off about."

"Joe Shaffer. And Shaffer was also the prosecuting attorney on the Junkins case, where your indictment came from."

"Correct," Frank Streets replied procedurally. "If you read this, and I don't want to put words in Joe Shaffer's mouth," he stated reluctantly, then cut himself off, visibly biting his lip. He stood up and walked to the back of his office again, grabbed another set of articles related to the Kelly case, all bound together.

Frank Streets stared at me for a moment then continued reading. "The West Virginia medical examiner has concluded it was a suicide. Our investigator clearly shows—now this is Lambert speaking," Frank Streets emphasized and then continued, "Our investigator clearly shows Mr. Kelly was murdered and it was not suicide." Frank Streets looked at me sternly. "Do your research on how a medical examiner produces a death certificate," he lectured. "They go by what the police tell them."

"Did the police say Kelly had no wounds?" I asked.

"No, the medical examiner was there in person," Frank Streets continued heatedly. "When he arrived at the scene, he went out and told the family we have a homicide. Then once the police got with him and they did all their talking, he changed it the next day to a suicide." He raised his eyebrows, as if to gauge my interest in the fishiness of the story.

"I spoke with the mother. She's the one that let him down. No open wounds on his arms, no cuts, nothing. Called the sister, she said she saw no marks. I called the medical examiner and recorded him. He said there were no open wounds on the body when he was there. He's the Harrison County coroner, so he pronounces him dead, ships him to Charleston for the autopsy."

Frank Streets's enormous frame swelled toward me over the desk. He whispered, slowly and heavily. "I get the death certificate back. It says the wrists were cut." He held the pause, letting it sink in. "So, I call the mortician. He's the one that embalmed him. He said there were no cut wrists." I listened intently, my heart beating quickly. "He said if the wrists were cut, he would have had to sew him up to keep the embalming fluid in." Frank Streets eyes widened as he looked at me. I inhaled very slowly and quietly, having held my breath for longer than I could remember.

"And the death certificate said the wrists were cut," I repeated suspiciously.

Frank Streets walked across his office and grabbed a copy of the death certificate to show me. I looked and could clearly see where someone had typed that the wrists were cut on the body.

"The mortician says the wrists weren't cut, but once I show him this," he shook the death certificate in front of me, his eyes great round orbs, his mouth open in perfect mimicry of my disbelief, "He says, 'I'm done. I see where this is going,' and he won't talk to me anymore." He tapped the typewritten words on the death certificate with his pointer finger. "So the only way to prove this? We're going to have to exhume the body," Frank Streets said with a straight face and perched on the edge of his seat as if he and I were about to run out to do just that.

"Jesus," I said, imagining a graveyard at night, Frank Streets digging madly in the pelting rain. He sharp teeth smiled wolfishly at me.

"But why would they, why would they lie?" I stopped, letting my face provide the shape of my confusion. "I mean, it all sounds strange, and maybe like a cover up, but why would the police want to murder this guy? And why would Shaffer want to hide that? It seems crazy."

"Here's the facts," he scowled at me, "and you need to do your own research." I laughed uncomfortably, trying not to blush after being scolded. "The dead boy, Michael Kelly, his fiancée's father is like a brother to Prosecuting Attorney Joe Shaffer. They're best of friends." He shifted in his chair. "I interviewed a bunch of people about it. The girlfriend was the last person to see him alive. She was seven weeks pregnant. She was there with her uncle about eleven o'clock that night. I called the uncle and he said he already talked to the prosecutor, and that he will not give a statement. People that don't give statements," Frank Streets muttered, leaning on the arm of his chair, "are hiding something."

He continued. "About six months prior to his death, Kelly was involved in an altercation. He and his fiancée were camping. Her dad and his brother—the uncle that was there the night Kelly died, who Shaffer advised not to speak with me—they nearly killed Kelly." Frank Streets quickly found a manila folder on his desk and removed a series of photographs. They were pictures of a young man in a hospital bed with his eyes swollen shut and his lips bluish and bulging like the flattened face of dead soldier strewn on a Civil War battlefield.

"Do we know what this altercation was about?"

"No, just that the father didn't want Kelly seeing his daughter." He paused thoughtfully. "I'll give you another public record, but you'll have to dig way back. When Joe Shaffer was a child, his father was in the mob in Clarksburg. His house was raided by the feds on Christmas Eve. That's public record," he repeated deliberately in the direction of my recorder. "Shaffer doesn't like the feds, and all the statements Sherman Lambert made started to get the attention from the feds, wondering if the prosecuting attorney's office is corrupt. That's what turned the heat on me."

I frowned. "So, the Junkins case, the Kelly case, your investigation of the sheriff—they're all connected." And the mob is involved somehow, too, I thought. I shook my head, feeling pity for Frank Streets. "And that's why Joe Shaffer would take the risk of creating false felony charges against you, to keep you quiet about everything you were finding."

"It's just speculation." I sensed some discomfort in the way he delivered that admission, and he looked at my recorder for the first time. "But it's damn good speculation, once you start connecting the dots."

"So why did your lawyer, why did Lambert recuse himself from your case?" My voice quavered. Frank Streets's eyes drifted again to the recorder I'd placed on his desk. I waited in silence, clenching my throat.

Frank Streets exhaled. "Four years ago," he began slowly, "I was working a murder case. Four co-defendants, Sherman Lambert had one, Paul Harris had one, two other lawyers had the other two. I was working with Paul Harris. The night before the trial, I'm here cramming and I get a phone call from a woman who is screaming. I don't know who it is, so I hit record. She says the state police just left her house, that they were threatening to take her kids from her, so she said she lied to them." We locked eyes, and I resisted the temptation to look down and away like usual, trying to match the intensity of his gaze, to hold him accountable to his truth.

"So, I asked her what in God's name she lied about." Frank Streets waited several beats. "She said she told them I gave her money to lie. She apologized, said I'm so sorry, I'm so sorry— but she didn't know I was recording her." I expected a smirk, but none surfaced on Frank Streets's face.

I was stunned. Frank Streets had been accused of bribing witnesses in a previous case, the same accusations leveled against him in his current felony charge.

"No charges were brought against me. It was over and done." He leaned back deliberately, his face taut. "Now, fast-forward to earlier this month at my hearing for my current charges, the prosecuting attorney presents the statements from that woman that called me." He raised an eyebrow in an attempt at coy suspicion, but his eyes betrayed his discomfort. "But that case was dropped," he protested immediately. "It didn't even go to court. It was an investigation, they came here, I cooperated, boom, boom, boom, no evidence," he said with as much impunity as he could muster, but his pantomimed gavel landed flaccidly.

I swallowed hard. I was still reeling from the discovery that this wasn't the first time Frank Streets had been accused of bribing a state witness. I thought about the adulterer we'd followed, how he'd cheated on his wife before, how he'd bought a cabin to make it easier, how his wife had convinced herself none of it was true.

I thought about Rex, how he had been abused before, and how eventually that pattern of abuse led to his death.

I thought about how I'd convinced myself that my life was conspiring against me, that being a husband and father was the reason I was failing to be the artist I imagined myself to be.

"They're trying to bring this in to make it look, you know," he cut himself off. "They can't. Because you gotta be charged. They didn't even charge me in that case. I never even went to court or nothing," he reiterated, his voice increasing in intensity as he leaned heavily on a critique of legal technicalities that made the prosecution's move inadmissible. Not once did Frank Streets deny that he did it. Maybe he felt he shouldn't have to.

"That's why Sherman Lambert left my case. Because his guy from that murder case with the four co-defendants was found guilty and he's appealing it, so Sherman's still representing him.

It's a conflict of interest for him to also represent me if they try to bring the accusations against me from that case into this one."

"If you're innocent, I say let them try to use those accusations," I challenged, sucking a breath slowly through my teeth.

Frank Streets nodded with a frown, his eyebrows raised. A look of concern briefly crossed his face. "But then again," he started slowly, "if they bring it in and this goes to jury, you may have some jury members say, 'Wait a minute, he's charged with this and four years ago they said he did this?' That won't look good," Frank Streets said, his face pushed upward in a facial shrug.

Poet Gregory Orr writes, "The devotee of conspiracy theories has an added edge of control—they have the power and knowledge to tell the 'true' story." Had Frank Streets really stepped on too many toes too often in his work as a PI, and now his adversaries were out to bring him down once and for all? Was he one of Auden's professional sleuths driven by ethics? Or was he an amateur out for his own good? He had made a good story of it; the pieces were all in place for it to be plausible. But it was also a strikingly familiar story: the hero private investigator framed for meddling with a corrupt justice system.

As a writer looking for a story about a PI's arrest, Frank Streets's conspiracy theory was too good to be true.

As a regular person talking with another regular person about why they were arrested, I had to conclude that it probably was.

As October made way to November and December, I called Frank Streets diligently every few weeks, talking more into his voicemail than to him.

I sent a Facebook friend request to the Barbour County sheriff. I'm still waiting for him to accept it.

I spent more and more time in the Blue Moose pecking away

at my computer and people-watching, obsessively editing what I already had written. It was an act of maintenance more than creation, and one that gave me relief rather than satisfaction, like when your lungs are on fire after being underwater too long and you gasp and go numb all over when you finally reach the surface. I felt hot with shame over the disparity between the fiction of who I wanted to be and the truth of who I was, how the time I spent working on this book with nothing to show for it was taking away from time I probably should have spent doing practical, useful things. Like vacuuming. Like doing laundry. Like planning meals and grocery shopping and paying bills. Like watching El instead of sending him to daycare, or getting a second job to supplement my meager income as an adjunct professor. I felt ashamed that I had created a conspiracy theory for my failure to be the artist I always believed myself to be that involved my wife and son. I felt shamefully privileged and irresponsible for tending to my fantasy of being a writer, especially when that fantasy relied almost entirely on K's support.

I was ready to unburden myself with Frank Streets and my failure to write a book about him and the fear of artistic irrelevance and middle-aged mediocrity it represented.

But if I did, it would confirm my fear that my identity as an artist was and would only ever be a fraud, an expression of my sheer egoism.

I wasn't ready for the story of Frank Streets to haunt me like a bewitched falcon from a preferred version of my life.

I thought about what it means to believe something is true as opposed to knowing it is, beyond a doubt, and just how much doubt can exist for something to remain believable. I thought about the varying degrees of deception lying requires, including the ones we tell ourselves before we can get others to believe them, wondering whether if all the little lies that line my interior were gathered and bagged and labeled as evidence they would amount to a more authentic portrait than any story they might be woven into, if the conspiracies we believe about ourselves are always true because of who they make us into.

Five years into my life in Morgantown, having forged an identity in feeling displaced, it felt too late to change. I'd given myself completely over to the notion that K and I would relocate following her loss of vision, and we were at the end of the timeframe I'd imagined for our departure. My life in West Virginia was supposed to have concluded by now. But it hadn't.

But that's not entirely true. Everything had changed. I had changed. I was in my mid-thirties, and I'd learned that time accelerates along an exponential curve. K and I had bought a house, gotten a dog, and had our first child. I worked more. I drank more. I slept less. I had gray hair on my chest and temples. My face was eroding into a topographical map. My eyes were sallow. I was losing hair on my knuckles and lower legs and growing it on my back and shoulders. I had two root canals and two crowns implanted in my jaw. I worried more and took fewer risks, in life and in art, having resigned that the two were separate.

I continued checking for updates on Blue Gray Ghost's blog, figuring he would have the inside scoop on the charges against Frank Streets since he had followed the developments in the sheriff's case so voraciously when it was breaking. But he had stopped posting anything. He hadn't written anything new on his site since I had left for Oaxaca. He hadn't even replied to the comments left on his previous posts, which was something he seemed to do no sooner than they had appeared on his blog for the three months leading up to his total internet silence.

I imagined conspiracies—he'd been paid off to be quiet, he was now a protected witness, the sheriff had knocked him off and buried him in Arden—but whatever it was, Blue Gray Ghost had dematerialized.

I had the urgent need to reveal the truth about something related to all these swirling stories and leads I had invested myself in. Blue Gray Ghost wanted to keep himself anonymous; if I could reveal the person hiding behind that mysterious little pen name, out him for the sport of it, then I would have accomplished something. I knew I was motivated by sheer ego, but I didn't give a shit. I didn't care how petty or irrational it was.

The day I visited Frank Streets and he revealed he had been accused of bribing and intimidating witnesses before, I mentioned Blue Gray Ghost to him, how I had been reading his incendiary commentary on message boards and his blow-by-blow analysis of the accusations against the sheriff on his blog.

"I've got a friend who says he definitely knows him," Frank Streets said with several rhythmic nods. "He said he sent word to say hello to me. I don't know who the ghost is and I don't want to know, and that's the truth. I don't want to know right now." He was thinking about the charges against him. "But evidently, he knows me, and I know him."

"He's plugged into the sheriff's department somehow," I suggested. "A sheriff's deputy maybe?"

"I've thought about that—and nah," Frank Streets said and frowned. "Can't be. The ones I know aren't this smart."

"Could he be a lawyer?" I asked again.

Frank Streets clutched his chin contemplatively. "Could be. I just don't know. My niece supposedly knows him personally. Matter of fact, just a couple weeks ago, when all this stuff was going down, she says, 'I've got something to tell you; you wanna know who he is?' and I said don't tell me nothing." His deliberate coyness was a posture for public display: let it be known Frank Streets was not interested in chasing real ghosts.

Unlike me.

"But, huh," I mused aloud, my own little show of coyness, "I just wonder what his name means," I trailed off, feigning benign curiosity.

"Well, Blue Gray is Civil War. And that's big here," Frank Streets said through a yawn. He looked at me like that connection was so obvious that he didn't even need to say it aloud. But he could sense my intrigue and continued. "We have the Blue Gray Festival every year because of the famous battlefield in Barbour County."

Given his dedication to injustice in Barbour County and nowhere else, it would make sense that Blue Gray Ghost was referencing the regional significance with his name. But that didn't reveal why he would reference the Civil War in a nom de plume dedicated to uncovering corruption.

A quick web search turned up that "Blue and Gray" were often used to describe the Union and Confederacy forces of the Civil War, respectively. I looked into the Blue and Gray Reunion in Philippi, West Virginia—the seat of Barbour County—and learned that it's a Civil War reenactment that inaugurates the reenactment season every year. Philippi is granted this honor because on June 3, 1861, it was the site of the first land battle of the Civil War, and the place has celebrated that history ever since.

I dug further, hoping Blue Gray Ghost had made a slip on the web that revealed his true identity. His blog was just a basic Wordpress template, and I hoped that meant he wasn't technologically savvy. I checked the "about" section on the blog. Nothing. I checked the admin tags on the bottom of his site to see if his username might give me a clue. It didn't. I checked what name his domain was registered under, but he had been smart enough to purchase privacy protection.

The only clue at all was the email address on his blog: JohnGrayGhost@hotmail.com. I googled "John Gray," thinking that might be his real name. Nothing. There was no profile information at all for that email address. My best guess was that it was a dummy email, and I wasn't sure how to find what address that email might forward to.

I googled "John Gray Ghost" and found that John S. Mosby, a Confederate Army battalion commander, went by the nom de guerre "The Gray Ghost," and operated in northern and western Virginia throughout the war. He'd earned his fame leading "Mosby's Raiders," a cavalry unit noted for its ferocious and speedy raids, eluding union forces and blending in with local farmers and townspeople. Legend had it that Mosby himself would don disguises and infiltrate union camps prior to his raids to gain an advantage. Master of deception and elusiveness, the Gray Ghost was a hero among the people who dwell in the mountains that form the border between Virginia and West Virginia.

It was a lead. There isn't much that Barbour County is known for other than its Civil War history and a couple of mummies displayed in the county courthouse, so why wouldn't my phantom blogger reference Mosby? And, if he was involved in the reenactments somehow, couldn't he know about Mosby—maybe he was a reenactor who dressed like Mosby and in so doing valorized his legendary elusiveness, his strategy of investigating his enemy in disguise to better bring his opposition to their knees before dissolving into the landscape?

I read an article in the *Inter-Mountain* that claimed the Blue Gray Reunion would return next year, which implied its continuation was in doubt. Given that it had been held for 150 years, this was a surprise. As I read on, the journalist mentioned that attendance to the event had dwindled in recent years and rumors had spread that it would be discontinued, but the co-chairman of the reunion vehemently debunked those rumors. The co-chairman.

I discovered that the co-chairman's name pops up all across Barbour and Harrison Counties. I found a LinkedIn profile for a person with that name living in Philippi. He was also a dispatcher for Barbour County 911. A dispatcher would hear every twist and turn of every investigation and case that came across his scanner.

I know who Blue Gray Ghost is.

But what does that say about me that I was so desperate to drag him out into the open? Maybe I wanted to uncover his identity because we were both writers orbiting the same cases. But our aims couldn't be more opposed. There's Blue Gray Ghost, an anonymous writer by choice, someone whose words are driven by a call to expose the worst in the world, to conjure something better through that work, and then there's me: a writer whose words are driven by the desire to make myself into a name that shows up on Google with a Wikipedia page, an author photo with a sparkle in my eye that convinces the world that I matter.

And I've always wanted to be smarter, better looking, more creative, and even more privileged than I already am. I've always wanted to become more valuable than the single point I occupy in a scatterplot of individuals who think and act and look and feel just like me, to transcend an entire generation of men taught to believe each of us is a unique snowflake against all evidence to the contrary, and entitled to a trophy because of it.

A 2012 study revealed that book authors' use of first-person-singular pronouns had increased in the previous decade while the plural forms had decreased, a symptom of our cultural shift toward the belief that each of our stories is more valuable than any story about us, a recurring proof that, in a period like our own, we sheer egoists are legion in America.

And I am a member of the generation raised to believe not only that each of our lives is important but also that each of our experiences and every story we have to tell about ourselves is meaningful enough to share.

And here, I am the bleeding heart of that generation.

I can only laugh at the irony of my anxiety about being unoriginal when all my thoughts and feelings are unoriginal—even my anxiety about being unoriginal being unoriginal—and my desire to transcend the influence of this age that has warped my perspective, to overcome my self-interest to instead value the people whom I love and who love me, have that be enough to fulfill me.

But I couldn't. I was resentful of the responsibilities K and El saddled me with. It seemed all the writers and artists I envied were cast in the mold of Franzen—they weren't married and definitely didn't have children. I wanted to travel and write and find success like them, be funny and unique and have all of my social media posts liked and starred and live the life of the beloved writer, and even as I could see how transparently that was an expression of my generational DNA, my resentment an expression of my Self-Made Manhood in crisis, I still couldn't purge it, I can't, like an addiction I was born with.

I slept at night by telling myself the support I gave both K and El every day was the debt to pay for my self-centeredness, how the sacrifices I made for the people I loved most were responsible for my unrealized aspirations.

I can't entirely acquit myself of the feeling that my failure is someone else's fault, and I look for others to blame.

I know who Blue Gray Ghost is.

And I have been shaped by the narrative that real men don't need help, that they just fucking get things done, and that the fact that I cannot ever get things done on my own means I'm not a man by that measure.

And I pick at the scabs of choices I've made, to dig for the potentials buried there.

If I didn't get married and follow K to West Virginia.

If I didn't have to live with my parents and commute to make it through college.

If I had taken the scholarship to study art in New York instead of going to school thirty minutes from home and a high school girlfriend.

If I hadn't had my first panic attack on the eve of turning ten, staring down the reality that people died in their double digits.

If I wasn't ruled by fear.

If I hadn't raged in the nursery when I was born, clawing at my face until it bled so badly that the nurse was forced to return me to my mother's embrace, and only there, finally, settling.

If I didn't always worry about purging my fears to make myself into something other than what I innately am, didn't put myself in situations that play to my weaknesses, hoping that just once I might overcome them.

To overcome my fears on my own, to make my own success,

do something important without needing help from others, to keep my struggles private.

Yet all I do is make pronouncements about the identity I wish was mine, a stage I should have grown out of.

As if I am in a coffee shop living life out loud, just hoping someone is listening.

As if that is self-evident.

Fuck books. Fuck art. Fuck the desire for petty and self-congratulatory measures of success. I am not strong, and I am not successful, and I am not a breadwinner.

Fuck all of it. I like being ordinary. I like doing laundry and cleaning and cooking. I like being a father.

Can I also be a man?

I don't have eccentric habits. Unless preferring to stay home and clean is eccentric. I like sports. I like mowing the yard.

Can I also be an artist?

I want to settle into what I am instead of being tormented by what I'm not, satisfied with my small and simple life. I want to be content with my truth.

"Believe it or not, the truth goes a long way in my book," Blue Gray Ghost acknowledges in the last post he ever published on his website. "More so than even the act in question. Why? Because it shows that while the person made a mistake, they can admit and own up to the mistake. That is of course how we as humans learn; by making a mistake and realizing where we went wrong and the first step is admitting that a mistake was made."

I am open to your judgment, dear reader. Please. This is my crisis of masculinity.

In December, a life-altering breakthrough occurred, one that I had been waiting years for. But it had nothing to do with art, or writing, or Frank Streets.

Of the dozens of applications K and I had submitted for jobs in other places over the years we'd been living in West Virginia, one finally paid off. K got invited to interview at a college in western New York, about thirty miles south of Rochester.

In Livingston County.

Fifteen minutes from where I was raised.

The same college I graduated from.

She got the job offer, and she accepted it.

We were leaving West Virginia.

Just like that.

For good.

And I want to say we were thrilled, that we hosted a week-long festival on our back deck celebrating K's new job because it marked our escape from West Virginia, the conclusion we'd been seeking all along. But it wasn't that clear cut for me. A return to western New York marked the masterstroke in a series of moves I'd started as a teenager who chose to remain there rather than chase my artist's dream of moving to New York City.

I'd spent my young life in Livingston County desperate to leave, and once doing that, I certainly never wanted to move back there. But my perspective had since tilted. I thought about the beautiful, privileged life that I had found in the regional obscurity of Iowa and then West Virginia while obsessing over myself and my failure to be anyone, anywhere else; I thought about K and El; I thought about Frank Streets; I thought about West Virginia, its history and people and how the two things that mattered most to me, my family and my art, were forever intertwined with them, and I was content with returning to western New York, soberly understanding what that meant for my identity.

I can't remember specific dates and times of important life events. I forget memorable details of places I've visited. Even the images I recall of places I've lived get dim as each colorful streak of my past swirls in a bucket until all is brown. So, when I say I don't remember when my mom first told me that her grandfather immigrated to West Virginia from Poland

and that her mother was born there, I do so honestly. I'd love to say it was when I called to tell her we were leaving West Virginia, that K and I were moving to live a short drive from my hometown, and I might as well, because that's the first time it mattered to me.

I had to drive south to the coalfields, to visit my family headwaters before I left West Virginia. I didn't have a clear plan for what I wanted to accomplish, just that I needed to see the place for myself, see where they worked, where they lived, to be present there.

I left before dawn, snaking south through the mountains, the early spring sun eventually rising over the ridges and casting curvilinear shadows along the contours of the landscape, penetrating the leftover winter grime on my windows to warm my neck and arms and pool in my lap. I drove past Fairmont and Clarksburg, past the exit that burrows into Barbour County toward Valley View Road; I passed signs for Shinnston, Jane Lew, and Lost Creek, my memories of those places a fresh swirl.

The sun on the dashboard flickered like a home-movie recording, reminding me of the long road trips my family would take to southern beaches for a week at a time to escape the chronic cold grays of winters in western New York. After hours spent heading in the same direction through familiar landscapes, when the buds finally appeared and eventually bloomed, the world I knew moved by in double-time, and I was a cursor dragged to the dark foliage that flashed from the dunes, the salty first taste of sea that marked the conclusion of our journey that suddenly felt so linear, so inevitable.

I drove through the mountainous terrain of central West Virginia, carving through the border of the Kanawha and Greenbriar Coalfields, into Fayetteville and the New River Coalfield, over another bridge that traverses the New River Gorge, and finally through Beckley, the Southern XXXPosure Gentleman's Club luring from the side of the highway with a host of tractor-trailers hunkered down in its vast parking lot.

After skirting the western edge of the Winding Gulf Coalfield, I entered the Flat-Top Pocahontas Coalfield, and at its heart, Pocahontas Mine, where my great-grandfather Peter Derring worked when as a young man he moved to Kyle, West Virginia, to begin his life in America.

Pocahontas Mine is now an exhibition mine with guided tours, but it was hard for me to imagine it as a bustling theme park; the town of Pocahontas has 441 permanent residents, and as I drove into it I saw none of them. Not one single moving car. Just a stack of still brick buildings and pavement riddled with potholes.

I had called the number on the Pocahontas Mine's website the day before to confirm it would be open, and the woman I'd spoken to on the phone had assured me it would be. The winter had been particularly harsh, and the mine had endured some ice and water damage that had delayed its opening. The woman remarked on my good luck: the day I'd selected at random to visit was the opening day of the tourist season.

I began to doubt her as I drove up to the mine's gaping maw. I expected to see a crowd of people waiting for the tour there, but as I looked around, I didn't. The mine loomed in front of me, a giant hole in the earth broad enough to drive a tractor-trailer into. No gate covering it. No sign saying keep out.

There was a warehouse adjacent to the mine, and the gravel chattered under my feet as I walked up and opened the door. The light cut across the concrete floor as I hesitantly poked my head into the interior of the cavernous warehouse. The space was dim and littered with cases of dusty mining memorabilia and black-and-white photos of miners, dirty and frowning like people in photographs from the early 1900s always seem to. I saw a woman at a glass counter standing beside an old-fashioned cash register. I greeted her cautiously, asking if the tour had started without me, and she assured me it hadn't. I gave her ten dollars—five for the tour and five for a two-gallon plastic bag filled with coal from the display case between us.

"When does the walking tour begin?"

The woman smiled warmly and gestured over my shoulder with her eyes. I expected to see a small group of people I'd somehow missed in a distant corner of the warehouse. Instead, I saw a bituminous chunk of a man walking toward me. This was my guide, a craggy-faced former coal miner well into his eighties who volunteered his time to the mine after years of working in it, like a captain who feels the tides pulling him to sea after his sailing days were behind him.

"Anyone else going on the tour?" I asked as he approached, already knowing the answer.

"Just you," he said gruffly as he turned slowly and began walking for the doors. There were no velvet ropes or turnstiles and no guards taking tickets, just the giant hole in the earth across from the parking lot that my guide walked slowly into, and I followed, the damp air dropping in temperature by twenty degrees a few paces in.

The tour was set up like a natural history museum, with a series of pits carved into the ten-foot-high walls to display the fossilized remains of ancient mine equipment. As we walked from pit to pit, my guide told me the story of the history of mining, letting me touch the canary cages and the wax candles, the small picks with wooden handles worn smooth from use, me breathless from the chance — remote, but still — that the one in my hand was once used by Peter Derring.

My guide led me by a series of wooden carts reinforced with steel, the kind that usually cut loose and careen in action movies with a shower of sparks, the hero wide-eyed and pathetically trying to influence its trajectory. He led me through the mechanized age of mining, the augers with their crocodile snouts that buzzed into coal seams with a ferocity that made Peter Derring and his generation into so many John Henrys. He lingered at the display of miners' trucks well after his explanation of them had ended, after he reached out and touched the miniscule cabin where the miners folded and stacked themselves for the ride down the shaft, like he had when he was a young man.

My guide stopped at one point and deliberately aimed his gaze at the mine ceiling directly above us. Imagine standing under a full-grown oak cast in stone and floating ten feet off the ground, the flight of branches obscured from view by the thick base and girders of roots that snake out radially from it. From that perspective, I didn't recognize the shadowy shape cast in relief in the stone above me as a tree. When my guide explained what I was seeing, I instinctually jumped to the side to get out from under it.

"Widow-makers," he explained, so named for the tendency of these petrified trunks and root systems to give way unexpectedly and bury miners under tons of rock. I already felt uneasy as we tunneled underground, and the widow-maker made me acutely aware that my feeling of safety was inversely influenced by my inability to fathom what was above me, a feeling similar to when I drive through manmade tunnels beneath mountains and channels, holding my breath as I expect my timing and luck to be the worst.

"How, what holds," I stammered, my mind searching for some practical explanation, some sensible reason that the tree could be contained intact after all these years, how it could float in stone, why it hadn't cut loose and collapsed, if it still might.

My guide stretched his arm toward the wooden jack bolted into the roof of the mine just to the side of the hard mass of roots above me. My eyes skipped along the sequence of jacks placed every twenty feet or so along the expanse of the tunnel, each about the same girth as a post that holds up a backyard deck.

I thought of the life I'd made in West Virginia, the fear of what I might have overlooked in my haste to leave.

I thought of K and El, the faith I had that they would hold for as long as I needed them to.

"That," he said looking at me, "is what holds up the mountains."

❆

Peter Derring made his first home in Kyle, twelve miles from Pocahontas Mine up, along, and over the ridge that separates them, and the drive there unfolded for me like an exit scene in need of credits. The road itself moved smoothly along a path carved by necessity, and while unlined, its switchbacks followed an internal logic. There were no guardrails even as the shoulders crumbled and vanished, the pavement invisible on either side of my car as I steered. After ten minutes of breathlessly driving up and then along the spine of a ridge the road eventually curled back down, my grip tight on the wheel and the arch of my foot cramping on the brakes as the road finally unspooled into a narrow corridor.

I imagined what it must have felt like for Peter Derring to land in New York City greeted by the *Statue of Liberty* and all it promised, and then days later to arrive in this landscape crowded with mountains and the smog of coal industry, bustling with smudged faces and dozens of unknown languages. I slowed as I entered Kyle, struck by the evidence of that time having passed long ago. My eyes skipped along the husks of buildings scattered alongside quiet railways with tall grasses sprouting between their weathered ties, viscerally aware of the still quiet when it was interrupted by the echo of a dog's bark or the distant wail of a train, the rumble in my belly as it steamed through the abandoned encampments that no longer demanded they stop.

I came upon a brief chain of windowless buildings. I pulled over to the side of the street. I got out of my car and walked the length of downtown Kyle, all of three blocks, surveying the very place where my great-grandfather lived as a young man, the mountains visible above the roofline on either side of me. And there are no statistics that capture how steep those mountains are, no way to quantify how mightily they press downward. Any data I could muster would be a disservice to the sense of isolation they invoke, the wedges of sky they begrudgingly provide, the way they level the fantasy of life rendered beyond the tunnel-view. If as a boy looking out the back window of my parents' minivan I imagined craning my neck enough to reach above the border of forest to see the world unfurl like an area rug, there was no way to imagine my neck extending far enough here.

And I wanted to discover more in Kyle, to find my grandmother's birth certificate in a little church, be helped by a spunky old woman who remembered hearing the echo of the name Derring, to have her take me to a plot of land that might have been where Peter and his family lived, to find a singed photograph of a man who looked like me holding a newborn in his smudged arms, to have it all coalesce in a meaningful story. But the church burned down decades ago. There was no little old woman. I saw only one man standing across from the gas station who smiled and waved at me both times I walked by him, but he bore no resemblance to me.

But even if I didn't find what I hoped to, I was still walking along the same street that my great-grandfather once had. Roughly one hundred years after he had arrived, I was seeing and feeling the same things as him.

I snapped a few pictures. I went to the bathroom in the gas station. I waved at the man who waved at me. I stayed five minutes at most.

Another thing I can't remember is when my mom first told me that Peter Derring committed suicide. When she told me about it on the phone the night before I drove to Kyle when I was picking her brain about my family's history in West Virginia, it struck me like it was the first time.

There weren't many details of his death known to her. It happened before she was born. Despite many of her aunts— Peter's children—still being alive, it was a story no one in the family talked about.

Still, a story was passed down somehow, the truth of which is suspect. My mom had always thought that he drank cleaning solution to kill himself, and when she told me this it sounded familiar, like I'd heard it before somehow as well. Then she heard he had hanged himself. Her aunt that found him was still alive, but she wouldn't talk about that day.

As a result, I know very minimal details of Peter Derring's fate: he moved to West Virginia; he married, had children; he moved his family to a farm in Virginia, the great success of his life; he moved his family to a farm in central New York and lost it all in the Depression, the great failure of his life; he committed suicide.

The rest is speculation. What if Peter Derring wasn't comfortable with all he had to give up to play the role of family man? What if he had a dream, too, and by midlife, he was disappointed and fed up and not as selfless as I would prefer to mythologize? What if all the men of that generation who gave themselves to their families, to their nation, to the betterment of the world did so reluctantly, and loathed every minute of it?

That story of a generation of men is more complicated and far less romantic than their ability to face down their failures stoically, quietly, as true Self-Made Men are expected to.

I considered digging further into Peter Derring's history to uncover his true identity: I would interview my ancient relatives to decipher the truth of why he killed himself.

To mine the seam of Peter Derring buried deep within me.

To better understand myself, my weaknesses, my struggle with sacrifice, and develop it into a grand argument about manhood and art.

But that process would just become my new, failed thesis, and I was wary of falling into the same old patterns as a way to define myself.

"The manhood of the future cannot be based on obsessive self-control, defensive exclusion, or frightened escape," Kimmel extols toward the end of his book. "We need a new definition of masculinity in this new century: a definition that is more about the character of men's hearts and the depths of their souls than about the size of their biceps, wallets, or penises; a definition that is capable of embracing differences among men and enabling other men to feel secure and confident rather than marginalized and excluded; a definition that centers on standing up for justice and equality instead of running away from commitment and engagement."

I believe as R. W. Connell does that "if patriarchy is understood as a historical structure then it will be ended by a historical process." In Connell's estimation, the practical problem facing a culture hoping to transform the structure that legitimizes patriarchy and breeds toxic masculinity is to cultivate pressures that lead toward awareness of the need for a change to occur. These first steps can be as humble as Self-Made Men admitting to their own failure, to their growing propensity for toxic expressions of manhood. "In early stages," she writes, "any initiative that sets up pressure towards that historical change is worth having."

Kimmel writes, "we need men who are secure enough in their convictions to recognize a mistake, courageous enough to be compassionate, fiercely egalitarian, powerful enough to empower others, strong enough to acknowledge that real strength comes from holding others up rather than pushing them down."

If there is a future for American men, it is in this form, the Other-Made Man.

And I know who Blue Gray Ghost is. I can name him here on the page with just a few quick keystrokes. But I won't.

It's the process of working toward who we desire to be that defines us, not the performance of it.

"In everything that can be called art there is a quality of redemption," Raymond Chandler writes of the writing he admires in "The Simple Art of Murder." "It may be pure tragedy, if it is high tragedy, and it may be pity and irony, and it may be the raucous laughter of the strong man. But down these mean streets a man must go who is not himself mean, who is neither tarnished nor afraid."

"This is practice," Eula Biss writes in *Having and Being*

Had. "And practice is all I want out of art." Not the conclusions we reach or the accomplishments we garner; not the identities we think those will create for ourselves.

A few weeks after I returned from Kyle, my phone rang in my pocket. I was driving to New York to look at houses with K and El, the sunlight a pinpoint refracting rainbows through the prism of my windshield.

"Hello?"

"This is Frank Streets."

"Hi, Frank!"

"You busy?"

"No, just driving—"

"See the paper yesterday?"

"No—I haven't—why, what's going on?"

"All the charges have been dropped."

"Wait—what?"

"Yep, it's in the papers. Just yesterday. Prosecution withdrew the charges against me."

"Why, how?"

"CJ's dead. Died of a heroin overdose. Seeing as his wife overdosed in September, they don't have any witnesses. It's over."

I had convinced myself I was okay never finding out the truth about Frank Streets until now that I couldn't.

"I did not accomplish what I set out to accomplish," Dyer writes of his failure to write about D. H. Lawrence in Oaxaca. "Except I could not accept that, could not abide by the consequences of that failure. The only way I could rectify things, it seemed, was to set out for Oaxaca on the first available plane. That was the only possible course of action. That is what I will do, I said to myself. I will go to Oaxaca. Immediately."

And I would go back to West Virginia to redeem my failure, to solve the riddle of Frank Streets, to find out once and for all if he was innocent or if he was a more accomplished storyteller than I would ever be.

I would go to the Blue Moose for one more cup of coffee, smile warmly at Dani and compliment her art, sit down with the self-conscious young woman with the headphones and listen to her.

I would go to Psychic Visions by Tina, the palm reading and tarot-card specialist whose storefront I'd driven by every time I went to visit Frank Streets, ask her what she could conclude about me.

I would have Bob Clay give me a lie detector test, to deduce what I actually believed and felt, to see what self-deception, if any, would be indicated in the stippled geography the needles left on the page.

I would interview Paul Harris and Sherman Lambert, observe them both in the courtroom.

I would track down the sheriff of Barbour County and question him mano a mano.

I would find Prosecuting Attorney Joe Shaffer, ask about the suspicious suicide and his connections to the mob, pin him to the precinct wall with a rhetorical chokehold, only releasing when I knew with certainty if the conspiracy against Frank Streets was true or not, if he is the man he believes himself to be.

I would drive to Valley View Road one last time to see Frank Streets.

I would take the photograph of him posing in his den that I always wanted.

I would buy one of his fox pelts.

I would treat him to the steak dinner I'd promised.

I would go on a ghost hunt with him, try and believe.

But in *The Maltese Falcon*, every character is damaged by the drive to find the Maltese falcon. It becomes a toxic obsession that ruins each one of them as they attempt to uncover its whereabouts. But the statuette they find is a fake; the "real thing" forever eludes them, leaving a wake of death, despair, and humiliation in its wake.

It doesn't matter if the entire world was conspiring to bring down Frank Streets or he had slipped a witness some money once or twice in his life. I would never find out the truth. And even if the conspiracy was a lie Frank Streets was telling himself—a lie that he believed about himself, a cornerstone of his identity, how he made himself the hero he wanted to be—then that made that conspiracy true, even if it wasn't.

As a kind of self-serving proof, a confirmation bias that invents its own logic as a means of survival, I could empathize. Frank Streets and I are the same in that way.

"I have one last question," I said into the phone and looked at K next to me, then in the rearview mirror at El in his car seat. "If I wanted to see some ghosts, which would be better to visit, the penitentiary in Wheeling or the Trans-Allegheny Lunatic Asylum?"

I pictured the grin sliding into place on Frank Streets's weary face. "Well, that depends. Do you believe in ghosts?"

"We've gone over this before! I just don't know."

"Me either!" Frank Streets answered honestly, my phone shaking with the thunder of his laughter.

"I don't disbelieve. I'm skeptical, though."

I would give up the chase of my Maltese falcon and be a better man for it.

"Even as I was filled with the power of this implacable resolution to make good on my previous mistake," Dyer writes, "I knew that I would not go to Oaxaca again, that I had no intention of going to Oaxaca, that of all the places on earth I might return to, Oaxaca was not one of them, that this determination to go back to Oaxaca was actually a way of coming to terms with not going to Oaxaca, was a way of atoning for my earlier failure by compounding it."

And I didn't go back to West Virginia. My earlier failure as a writer was to think that if I got to the bottom of other people's lives it would reveal something about me.

And my earlier failure as a man was to think that being a husband and a father wasn't something I could be proud of. "I cannot accept myself as I am," Dyer concludes, "but, ultimately, I am resigned to accepting this inability to accept myself as I am." I am not the artist I wanted to be, and I am not the family man I believe I should be, but at the bottom of it all I am some part of both.

But even if I didn't go back to West Virginia, there have been two times in my life I have gone back to make good on something: once in Kyoto when I dragged K back to the garden we had just left after sitting in it together for ten minutes in comfortable silence, vibrating with the waves of sand in the Crane and Tortoise Garden when I realized it was the place to give her the ring in my pocket; and once in Oaxaca, when I dragged El back to the market artist the day before we left to buy an etching he made of a father playing a violin, and his son playing a fishbone, standing side by side with their eyes looking up to the sky.

If this is failure and my manhood is defined by it, then may we all fail so well.

THANKS TO

The people and places of West Virginia.

The writers and artists referenced in this book.

Ben and Sally: Morgantown will always be ours.

Libby VanWhy: you designed a dream cover, pal.

Jeremy B. Jones and Torrey Peters: you challenged me to make this book do and be more.

Jennifer Huang: you brought this book to the public and helped me find its readers.

David Oates and Scott Parker: you believed in my perspective and gave me the license to make this book the one I always imagined, inside and out.

Frank Streets: you let me tag along when you had no good reason to. I will chase ghosts with you anytime.

Mimi and Elliott: you remind me every day how and why this whole thing got started.

My parents: I am not the man I am without you showing me the way.

Karleen, my most trusted reader, invaluable editor, diehard fan, and all-time favorite partner-in-crime: you believe in me and what I can do even when I don't. Thank you for that gift.

FRANKLIN D. STREETS
is an investigator, polygraph examiner, and former
sheriff's deputy who lives in West Virginia.

STEPHEN J. WEST
is a writer, teacher, and parent who previously
lived in West Virginia.